From Beginner
to Expert

Sebastian Höher

Unicycling

With photos by Heinz Karstädt
and illustrations by Anna Bade

Translated by Wayne Middlemist

The author would like to express his special thanks to Eckhard Euen, Adrian Voßkühler, Anja Geißler, Philipp Sünderhauf, Angela Luce-Höher, Ditta Ruppenthal, Wulf Karstädt and Claus Paetzold.

Published by Butterfingers
Bath, January 1994
© 1994 Butterfingers
All rights reserved
The original edition was published
under the title EINRADFAHREN
in the series rororo sport
Copyright © 1991 by
Rowohlt Taschenbuch Verlag GmbH,
Reinbek bei Hamburg, July 1991
Picture credits: see page 174
Typesetting by
Create Publishing Services Ltd. Bath
Printed and bound by The Bath Press
ISBN 0 9513240 5 5

A C.I.P. catalogue record for this title
is available from the British Library

Contents

Basic Techniques of Unicycle Riding   50

Starting Off   50

Learning with Help   52

Learning to ride alone   59

Riding the unicycle   61

Introduction

This book is intended for children and adults alike, both girls and boys, and women and men. It explains the basic and advanced techniques of riding both standard and tall (Giraffe) unicycles and explains how to learn these techniques. The book describes the most important ways to mount and ride a unicycle, and encourages you by means of over 100 practice exercises and coaching tips to try them out and to learn them yourself. The large number of techniques and practice exercises described in this book also ensures that even in the long term you will not get bored with your unicycling, and that in the course of time the riding and practising will lose none of its fascination. The book is organised and written in such a way that anyone can learn to unicycle. In addition to the main section of the book, which traces the path from beginner to expert, many other topics are covered which are of interest to unicyclists. These include equipment and safety, some aspects of the movements to be learned, how to juggle on a unicycle, how to ride tall unicycles (Giraffes), and the physics and history of unicycle riding.

Unicycling is the most pleasurable form of cycle riding - but also the most demanding. In describing the most essential techniques, and through its tips and suggestions, this book will be a great help towards mastering the art of unicycle riding. Only through practice, however, will you make the decisive step to success.

If you want to ride a unicycle well you must employ your best qualities when learning and practising: enthusiasm, skill and perseverance.

Why Unicycle?

Since the invention of the bicycle people have taken to riding on two wheels. You can learn to ride a bicycle quickly and even after just a little practice you can stop yourself from toppling over. A bicycle equipped with lights and mudguards is a good means of transportation, even at night and in rain. Changing gear enables you to save energy when pedalling. The handle-bars enable you to control the direction of the bike - they can be also be comfortable to lean on as you cycle along. Finally, you can carry all sorts of things on a bicycle.

Unfortunately a unicycle offers none of these advantages. On the contrary, it is the most unstable machine you can imagine. There are no lights or mudguards, and since you are unable to change gear, saving energy by pedalling slower is out of the question. A unicycle is also unsuitable as a means of transport. So of all things, why unicycle?

1. Unicycling is fun. It is fun to continually defy gravity and appear to confound the laws of physics.
2. Unicycling is a challenge. It is a challenge to master the most difficult form of cycling. A challenge, to ride confidently on a unicycle through your own persistence and skill. It is fun once you learn how to do it and it can be as interesting and enjoyable as mastering other types of sporting apparatus, such as a surfboard, a skateboard, a pair of skis or a sailing-boat.
3. In sporting terms, unicycling offers a great deal. It is excellent for the development of concentration and co-ordination and can also be good training for strengthening the legs. Your sense of balance becomes more pronounced. This makes unicycling complementary to other types of sport for which the above mentioned qualities are a prerequisite.

Champion Skier Armin Bittner

So windsurfers are able to develop their sense of balance on land during 'windless' days. It can also be good policy for skiers and ice-skaters, who want to be prepared for the season, to train with the help of a unicycle by practising strength and co-ordination exercises. These exercises can also be part of summer training.

4. Unicycling, like other forms of sport, is one in which a certain level of skill or mastery can be attained. After suitable practice you will master different tricks on the unicycle and ride it in a smooth, relaxed, effortless and entertaining way. The time you spend practising on the unicycle as you progress from beginner to expert will not be boring, for your qualities of coordination are constantly being challenged.

5. Unicyclists are winners. Organised competitions in which it is possible to lose are of little interest to unicyclists. Whereas in other types of sport people are often competing against each other, with unicycling such competitiveness is the exception. The insignificance of competition does not, however, mean that ambition in unicycling is stifled - in fact quite the opposite. Unicyclists neither want to 'defeat' anybody, nor be 'defeated'; they want to improve through the fun of practising and to gain satisfaction from their skill. In this way they win, but not at the expense of making others losers.

6. Unicycling is easier than it first appears, and with suitable instruction and practice anyone can do it. Riding forwards a few metres on a unicycle is about as difficult as it is for a small child learning to ride a bicycle without stabilizers.

7. Apart from toddlers, riding a unicycle can be learnt at any age. Regardless of whether you are a child, a teenager or an adult, your desire to learn is the most important factor, not your age.

8. Unicyclists do not need to be members of a club, nor do they need to keep to any fixed training schedules and locations. They ride and practise when they have the time and desire to do it.

9. Unicycling is relaxation through concentration. What actually sounds like a contradiction is in fact not the case. The concentration required to maintain balance initially demands your complete and undivided attention. Relaxation is achieved during this process because your everyday thoughts are blanked out.

Unicyclists are marvelled at and admired throughout the world for their great skill and inventiveness.

There are certainly other reasons behind the appeal of unicycling. In comparison to a standard bicycle you have more options; you can make sudden changes of direction, ride backwards and bunny-hop on a unicycle; you can use your free hands to juggle; hopefully, the balance that you attain externally can also develop your inner balance and you can be sure that this form of cycling is an environmentally friendly activity.

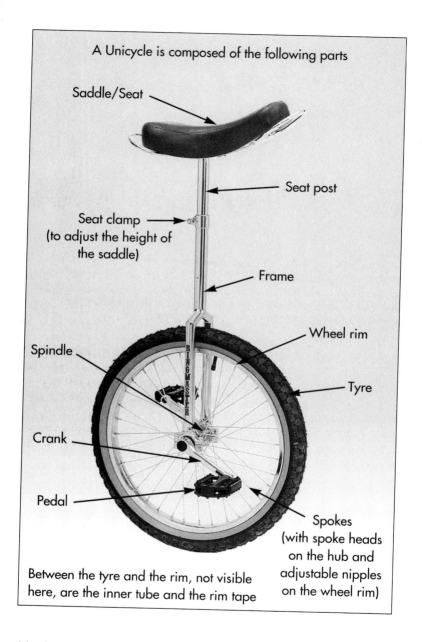

A Unicycle is composed of the following parts

Saddle/Seat

Seat post

Seat clamp
(to adjust the height of
the saddle)

Frame

Wheel rim

Spindle

Tyre

Crank

Pedal

Spokes
(with spoke heads
on the hub and
adjustable nipples
on the wheel rim)

Between the tyre and the rim, not visible
here, are the inner tube and the rim tape

14

The Right Equipment

This section provides information about the unicycle as a piece of sporting equipment. It gives a brief overview of the mechanics of the unicycle and describes all the current variations in unicycle construction. Since unicycles are made worldwide in many and varied forms it is not possible to mention or discuss all the different makes.

With standard unicycles the cranks are located directly on the spindle. Unicycles on which the saddle and pedals are so high that the wheel is driven by a chain connected to the spindle are described as tall unicycles, more commonly as Giraffes (p.132ff). Unicycles which have neither frame nor saddle are known as 'Ultimate wheels' (p.134). Any other machine which normally has more than one wheel in contact with the ground and is operated by muscle power is not, of course, a unicycle.

The unicycle:
A versatile machine

New unicycles can be purchased from shops which cater for circus and juggling needs, possibly from large, well-equipped bicycle shops or directly from the manufacturer (see Appendix for list of addresses). Second-hand unicycles are best sought through other unicyclists or sometimes via classified advertisements.

With unicycles, as with all technical products, there are differences in quality and design. The size of the wheel is the most important feature, for it has a decisive effect on riding behaviour.

The most common wheel sizes are 16″ (for children under 10 years of age), 20″ and 24″.

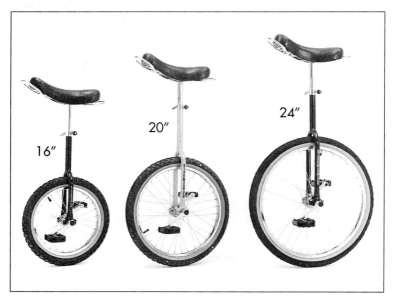

Unicycles come in a number of different wheel sizes. The size is given in inches ("), one inch equalling 2.54 cm. The specifications correspond to the diameter of the wheel. A 20" wheel has a diameter of approximately 50.8 cm and a circumference of 159.6 cm. Since (almost) every unicycle has a 1:1 gear ratio, one complete revolution of the crank with a 20" wheel will cover 159.6 cm.

The wheel size has a decisive influence on the way the unicycle handles. The smaller the wheel, the more manoeuvrable the unicycle. However, the smaller the wheel, the faster you have to pedal, although the pedalling is less strenuous. In contrast a large wheel is less manoeuvrable; you need more space and the pedal motion is more energy-sapping. On a 16" unicycle you make approximately 78 complete revolutions of the cranks to travel 100 metres; on a 26" only 48. The following comparisons between a standard bicycle with gears and the effort required to pedal a unicycle can be made: 1st gear on a bicycle = 16" wheel on a unicycle; 2nd gear = 20"; 3rd gear = 24"; 4th gear = 26"; 5th gear = 28" (Siegmon unicycle). The range of wheel sizes offered by the various manufacturers includes, among others, the following: 12", 16", 18", 20", 24", 26", 27", 28".

Here are some further differences in the manufacture of unicycles:

Saddle
It is most important that you can sit comfortably on the saddle for long periods. For this reason it is suggested that you spend some time trying out the saddle when buying a unicycle. If you cannot ride one yet, bring some friends along to support you on the saddle while you test it. Very cheap saddles do not always endure heavy usage well and frequent falls can result in premature wear and tear. A saddle which is a little wider at the front and back is known as a contoured saddle. Contoured saddles generally provide a good sitting position and good support. Very flat saddles (T-bar saddles) are less kind to your backside, though all the riding techniques in which you hold the saddle as you ride along (see pages 115 ff) are easier. Some saddles have metal loops at the front and back.

These loops are useful for catching or holding the unicycle and protect the saddle from damage in the event of a fall.

Seat post

Several fastening points make the connection of the seat-post with the saddle more secure. The height to which the saddle can be adjusted is determined by the length of the tubing.

Seat clamp

An infinitely adjustable seat clamp guarantees a saddle height to suit the rider. However, with heavy use or substandard workmanship this clamp can slip or twist. A seat clamp which clicks into position, or one secured by holes is not infinitely adjustable, but on some unicycles the height can be adjusted at intervals of 2.5 cm. This should be sufficient to find the right sitting position and it will not slip or twist.

Frame

Technology offers the option of either solid or divisible frames.

Cranks

A square crank is a better option than a cotter-pin - the connection is more robust and durable. Which type of crank can be attached depends on the spindle. The length of the crank also affects the riding characteristics of the unicycle. With a long crank each turn of the pedals describes a wider circle and is consequently more energy-efficient. A shorter crank, however, is less energy-efficient, though you pedal faster because of its smaller turning circle.

Pedals

Apart from a few (children's) makes, most pedals contain ball-bearings. The durability and load capacity of the pedals depends on the quality of these bearings. For unicycles large rubber block pedals with non-slip tread are suitable.

Spindle and spokes

Ball-bearings are the key to the quality of the spindle. If they are well-protected from dirt and dust the life-expectancy of the spindle is prolonged. Whether the (brake-) forces will have more of an effect on the spokes or the spindle depends on how the spokes are organised between the spindle and the wheel rim, i.e. how often the spokes inter-cross each other. On a standard spoked wheel (1 to 4 cross) enormous stresses act on the spindle via the spokes. Therefore the stress is bigger the more often the spokes cross each other. A configuration in which the spokes do not cross at all is described as radial spoking. In this case the stresses on the spindle are smaller, those on the spokes greater. The less the spokes cross each other, the more load weighs on the spokes and in particular the spoke heads, which in extreme cases can break.

Wheel rim

Wheel rim widths range from very narrow 1 1/4" rims to 1 3/8" (Dutch size) and 1.75" (Normal touring size), up to very wide rims of 2.125" (Mountain bike size). The usual width for unicycle rims is 1.75".

Tyres

As flat a tread as possible is recommended to give a smooth ride. A totally worn tyre, i.e. a treadless one, is often felt to be quite pleasant. Tyres with very heavy tread produce a slight vibration as you go along, and are suited to outdoor use. Bright or colourful tyres are more suitable for riding on gym floors.

In addition to standard models, some manufacturers also offer custom-built unicycles, so you can order your unicycle as an individually assembled 'work of art'. If you do not want to ride a standard unicycle, here is an example to stimulate your imagination:

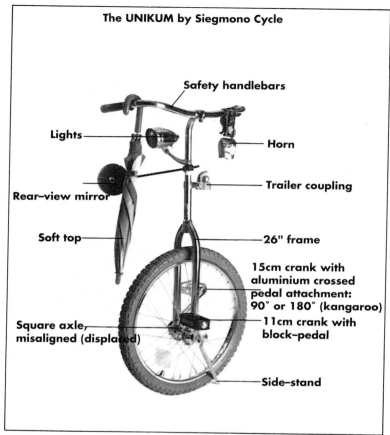

The UNIKUM by Siegmono Cycle

Safety handlebars

Lights

Horn

Rear-view mirror

Trailer coupling

Soft top

26" frame

15cm crank with aluminium crossed pedal attachment: 90° or 180° (kangaroo)

11cm crank with block-pedal

Square axle, misaligned (displaced)

Side-stand

Unikum

If you have a talent for tinkering you can build a standard or wacky unicycle yourself. Anything goes here (almost), for when building a unicycle there is only one restriction: Only one wheel may be in contact with the ground. Where and at what height the saddle is, whether the spindle is attached to the centre of the wheel or misaligned with it, whether you attach one crank or two - the choice is yours.

Gyro Gearloose demonstrates something which not every designer manages; building an unusual unicycle and actually being able to ride it.

21

Choosing the right unicycle

Before buying your unicycle, it is advisable to be certain about the following questions:

1. What do I want to do with the unicycle?
2. Which wheel size is most suitable?
3. How much does a unicycle cost?
4. Is my height and weight suited to every unicycle?

1. For occasional use you do not need to buy an expensive or particularly robust unicycle; the most inexpensive basic model should suffice. If you feel, however, that you might be seized by the unicycle bug, go for a more solid and probably more expensive one.

2. A 16" wheel is suitable for children; for adult beginners a 20" or a 24". It is slightly easier to ride with a 20" wheel when starting off, and since it is smaller you are nearer to the ground and you will feel more confident. However, with the smaller wheel the ride is rather choppy. Buy a 24" wheel if you want to cover longer distances and you place a value on a smooth ride. If you are only able to practise in a small room go for a small, manoeuvrable wheel. Developing the leg muscles is best with a bigger wheel.

3. Cheaply imported unicycles, (mostly) from Asia, can sometimes be purchased for little more than half the price of those regarded as well-built from European manufacturers. Since prices are constantly changing, it is worth making enquiries with the manufacturers and distributors.

4. For children or lightly built people a unicycle with 28 x 2mm thick spokes should be sufficient. For adults the unicycle should be equipped with 36 spokes. For particularly heavily built people strengthened spokes (2.34 mm; 2.6mm) are available. When sitting on the saddle you must be able to place one foot comfortably on a pedal at the bottom of its turning circle. If this is not possible with the saddle in its lowest position, you should buy a smaller unicycle.

These two have found the right unicycle for their height.

Adjusting the unicycle

To adjust the unicycle correctly you must establish the correct height of the seat post. This is when you sit upright on the saddle with the sole of the foot on the pedal, and with the knee-joint almost completely outstretched when the pedal is in its lowest position. Some unicyclists prefer to place the ball of the foot on the pedal, giving them particularly good control. It is not a problem if the saddle is too low in the early stages - the issue is more about learning to ride than achieving style points.

The saddle is at the right height when, with the pedal in its lowest position, your leg is almost outstretched.

However, provided it is not a problem, you should practise with the saddle at the correct height so that you do not grow accustomed to a style which saps your strength and looks slightly awkward. More advanced unicyclists can experiment a little with the adjustment, for example by fixing the saddle in its lowest position and 'duck-walking'.

Clothing

If you can ride confidently and you are not riding for too long, standard everyday clothes are fine for unicycling. For longer periods, however, you should consider your choice of clothing more carefully.

The choice of clothing is particularly important at the point at which there is continual contact between rider and unicycle. Since these points are the feet, the backside and the inner thigh, you are recommended to wear the correct footwear and trousers. Sports shoes with a good grip are quite suitable, but the soles should not be too thick. The shoelaces should not be too long as they can get caught up in the wheel, or, in the case of a Giraffe unicycle, in the chain. Only when you can ride well should you wear gym shoes with an extremely thin sole. Cycling shorts with sewn-in seat padding are also suitable. This padding is made either from a special synthetic material or from leather. No underwear is worn under cycling shorts, for after a while you quickly find that the thread of the underwear slowly but surely works its way into your flesh. You will then be forced to take a break for a while.

A very long T-shirt hanging outside the trousers around the saddle can cause difficulties when you try to catch the unicycle as you dismount.

Gloves can be also be useful if at certain stages you will be making frequent contact with walls, fences and floors etc.

Maintenance

Depending on the frequency and the way in which it is used, a unicycle, like other sporting equipment, will require care and maintenance. Some of the parts are prone to normal wear and tear.

Apart from the tyre, the pedals and the seat cover are the most vulnerable, especially when you are learning. If you do not hold on to the unicycle when you fall off, these parts are particularly affected and will have to be replaced from time to time. The seat cover can be removed quickly and replaced with a new one. You will need a few minutes to change a pedal. An open-ended spanner is required, as flat and as long as possible, size 15 mm. Both the cranks and pedals are marked with the symbols (R) and (L) - these must match with each other. When attaching the pedals to the cranks make sure they are secured firmly - if they are loose the stresses applied to the pedals and cranks when mounting and riding the unicycle can damage the thread. To change a broken crank use a crank puller by screwing it into the spindle end of the crank.

Particular attention should be given to the tyre. Since the pedals are usually in the same position when you change direction, the tyre is worn unevenly on a (chainless) unicycle with a mandatory 1:1 gear ratio. This means that after a while (depending on the roughness of the floor) two points on the tyre will be heavily worn in comparison to the rest of the tyre. So that you are not constantly replacing worn tyres you are recommended to move the tyre a quarter-turn before it gets completely bald. To do this, let the air out of the tube and loosen the tyre from the wheel rim so that it can be moved. After a quarter-turn fix the tyre into the rim again and inflate the tube. This way you prolong the life of the tyre.

A brand new unicycle will usually ride perfectly smoothly, as the spokes are all tightened equally by the manufacturer. However, with use the uniformity of the spoke tension can be distorted, in extreme cases so much so that the wheel buckles. You can detect this either by observing the wheel as it spins or by using a centring device. This can be obtained from bicycle accessory shops. With the help of a centring device you can remove a buckle from the wheel; the apparatus tells you exactly which spokes have to be tightened and by how much. Most bicycle shops will do this for a small charge.

If the unicycle is ridden vigorously the stresses on the spokes can cause them to break. This usually occurs due to sharp braking forces, which weaken the spoke heads located on the spindle. Such forces arise, for example, when suddenly going from riding forwards to hovering. If you want to avoid a buckle in the wheel, you should replace a broken spoke immediately. The correct tension of the new spoke can be established by testing the tension with the fingers or by ear. Gently tap the spokes with a screwdriver; spokes of the same tension produce the same sound.

The chain on a Giraffe should be kept clean and dry. Since you frequently make contact with the chain when you mount a Giraffe unicycle, it is in your interest to grease the chain sparingly.

The unicycle and all moving parts should be cleaned a little every now and again.

So that you do not have to march off to the shop every time you have a small technical defect, you are recommended to keep some tools and replacement parts handy. This will prove particularly useful when something breaks at the weekend or on holiday and you are a long way from the nearest bike shop.

PARTS

- Valves
- Inner tube
- Tyre

- Cranks
- Pedals
- Bicycle pump

- Seat cover
- Spokes with nipples

TOOLS

- 15 mm open-ended spanner for removing and fastening the pedals
- Tyre lever for changing the tyre
- Spoke spanner for adjusting spoke tension
- Crank puller for removing the cranks

Safety First

Falls, clumsy dismounts and sometimes unintentional clowning are unfortunately part and parcel of being a beginner. Even more advanced unicyclists, practising new tricks, will have to dismount more often than they would like. Those advanced unicyclists who no longer have to dismount have either reached perfection or are not riding to their limits and therefore will improve only moderately. Since, however, falling off is very much a part of unicycling - only the moment when is unknown - certain safety precautions can be taken in advance.

Avoiding injury

Heavy falls on a unicycle are rare, and the injuries which may result are usually minor. There are no statistics on the frequency of particular unicycle injuries, though it is known from bicycle riding that the head (19%), lower extremities (25%) and upper extremities (40%) are the areas most vulnerable to injury.

Head injuries are basically rare in unicycling and threats to your health are likewise less likely because of the lower speeds. To avoid most injuries it is important to know that sometimes when falling off you can still briefly steer the unicycle. If you fall forwards or backwards in the direction of travel, the unicycle usually slips away from you and you can land on your feet.

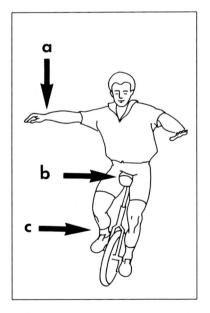

Vulnerable areas of the body

The following areas are at most risk of injury when unicycling:

a: Upper extremities
b: Pelvic area
c: Lower extremities

Upper Extremities

You often use your hands to break a fall. On rough ground this can cause abrasions. In bad cases a particularly heavy fall may result in a sprained wrist.

You also risk injury to the hands by reaching out for a wall, a fence, a tree or a lamp post to try and stop yourself falling. Finger injuries can result when you fall off the unicycle and try to prevent it from hitting the ground by grabbing the saddle. If you have a saddle with metal loops you can catch the fingers in the gap between the loop and the saddle itself.

To avoid injury to the hands it can be helpful, particularly when learning, to wear old gloves made of leather or some other robust material.

Pelvic area

Most minor injuries to the upper inner thigh usually occur when you attempt to grip the saddle as you fall or when you grip the saddle between the thighs for bunny-hopping without using your hands. Frequent mounting and dismounting can likewise pinch and chafe the skin in the pelvic area.

The genitals can also be injured when unicycling. Whereas females suffer less from such injuries, males risk crushing their testicles when over-zealously mounting the unicycle, or they can be bruised when sitting on the saddle. Not a matter of life and death - you can usually stand up again immediately - but it is unpleasant and painful, if not a little inelegant.

Tight cycling shorts with seat-padding come in handy here. The scrotum can be hitched up a little higher and the padding is comfortable to sit on and kind to the skin. If the shorts have a leather insert, it should be greased with a special cycling cream. The leather and the skin are thus preserved and chafing is largely prevented. Cycling shorts with synthetic padding guarantee optimum hygiene through permanent anti-bacterial protection. If you still have problems in this area, contact with the unicycle saddle can be avoided for a while by practising techniques in which you hold the saddle rather than sit on it (see pages 115-118).

Lower extremities

You can quite often bruise your inner anklebones, particularly in the early learning stages. If you do not place your feet correctly on the pedals, the anklebones make contact with the cranks every time the wheel goes round. In a nutshell, this is *the* unicycle injury. If you are unable to solve the problem by placing your feet more to the outside of the pedals (step 1), you should wear ankle-high sports shoes (step 2). If you still have difficulties, use padded ankle supports (step 3). Another possibility is to use tape; in extremely persistent cases you can reinforce the tape with layers of material, pieces of felt, bits of rubber etc. by attaching them to the self-adhesive side and taping it directly over your ankles (step 4). If that also proves of little use you can play safe and avoid pain by having your feet put in plaster (step 5).

With some falls a pedal may hit your shinbone or calf with considerable force. The calves are vulnerable to the cranks when travelling forwards, though this is less painful because the muscle acts as padding. However, when the cranks are turning in the other direction, i.e. when you are going backwards, the shinbones are particularly vulnerable to being hit by the pedals if you fall - not a pleasant experience. If you hold the trailing leg in the wrong position when learning to ride or hover with one leg, for example, it can be struck by the free pedal.

Since in damp weather the danger of the tyre slipping on the ground and of your feet slipping on the pedals increases, you are advised not to ride outdoors in such conditions. Riding barefoot on a unicycle is not a good idea - certainly when learning you should always wear sturdy and, if necessary, ankle-high sports shoes with good grip but not too thick a sole.

For safe unicycling it is also important to choose the right place to practise and to observe safety distances.

32

Where can you unicycle?

In most countries everything is fairly well regulated. Officially, you are not usually permitted to unicycle on roads and cycle paths. Strictly speaking this also applies to public footpaths because unicycles are not classified as pedestrian traffic. Some countries do not even classify unicycles as bicycles and therefore they are not to be used in public places. Rather, they are classified as pieces of sporting equipment which, like others, should not be used on public thoroughfares where they might obstruct or endanger the public.

Experience shows that if you give some impression of control and safety, unicycling is tolerated by the police on suitable cycle tracks and footpaths. Cycle tracks and footpaths are suitable if they are flat and wide, are not busy and have few obstacles. Basically it depends on whether you meet a policeman who can see the sense of fun in unicycling. My experiences with the police have been positive. The range of police reaction varies from fairly light-hearted observations regarding the lack of lights and brakes to appreciative applause.

Roads with normal motor traffic are to be avoided for three reasons:

1. Even good unicyclists can quickly find themselves under the wheels of a car. Drivers are often confused by unicycles, react unpredictably, do not on the whole keep safety distances and rarely take unicyclists into consideration, if at all.

2. Drivers can be so captivated by the skill of unicyclists that they cease to pay attention to other traffic. This may lead to accidents.

3. Unicycling on the road is quite simply illegal in most countries. The police do not usually tolerate it in the way they tolerate riding on cycle paths and footpaths (strictly speaking also illegal).

Practice Space

Beginners need as smooth a floor as possible (asphalt car parks, gym floors etc) and something handy to hold on to, like a fence, a wall, a door frame, gym wall bars or a window sill. If you are learning to ride a unicycle with one or more helpers, or you can already ride one, you need only a flat surface and an open space.

A gymnasium is an ideal practice space, though few people will have the opportunity to use one. Good places to practise are empty car parks, the end of little used cul-de-sacs, asphalt paths in parks or quiet, level footpaths next to a house wall or a fence.

Avoid practising on very rough ground in the early stages. It reduces the life of the tyres and the risk of injury in the event of a fall is greater. Do not cycle on damp ground - likewise the danger of falling and of injury increase in such conditions. Bumpy and undulating terrain, and anything lying on the ground such as twigs and autumn leaves, are all the curse of the novice unicyclist.

If you are out practising and you come across motorised traffic, the maxim is always as follows: dismount and wait for it to pass before you carry on again.

It is also possible to practise at home, though unfortunately damage to the wallpaper, the walls, the furniture and particularly carpets and other floor coverings is often the result. Few neighbours are happy to hear the sound of a unicycle clattering to the floor.

In showing the appropriate restraint by not practising at home, there are, however, two cases in which you can do it with a clear conscience:

- Beginners can practise balance exercises on the unicycle in a doorway.
- The more advanced can practise tried and tested techniques which do not require a large area under optimum conditions (large room on the ground floor with little furniture, a hard-wearing floor surface and no neighbours - or deaf ones).

It is stupid, though appealing to an audience, to ride on the edge of steep overhangs, on high walls or on parapets. One mistake here means the end of your unicycling career.

Although strictly speaking illegal, unicyclists can also join in with other users of cycle paths and footpaths (not on roads) to go to school or work, for example, or to go shopping. It is essential, however, that you can ride confidently, can change direction and speed, can do a free-mount and keep hold of the unicycle when you dismount. Before you venture among other pedestrians and cyclists, test your proficiency with the exercise on page 69.

Keeping a safe distance

With some unfortunate falls the unicycle can fly off quite a distance. My record is over six metres. Objects struck by a unicycle can be damaged or completely demolished, as can the unicycle itself. To avoid this, it is to your advantage to keep a minimum distance from other objects and people.

When riding without support in the early stages you should keep a distance of at least 3 metres from other objects. When riding backwards, or when riding a Giraffe, this distance should be doubled. In your own interest you are advised not to cycle too close to parked vehicles as a moment's loss of concentration can prove very expensive.

> The more risks you take and the higher you sit on the unicycle, the greater the safety distance should be.

The last thing beginners need is to be subjected to the mental pressures of annoying and misplaced advice. If this happens, you would be well-advised to keep a safe distance from the sort of nuisances who give it. A sincerely intended "No, no, not like that, I knew someone once who did it differently" is certainly still palatable; likewise a sneering "...Ah, you're still a beginner" at a pinch; finally, with an insistent "Let me have a go, I can do that too...", it may be better for all concerned if you look for a quiet, unobserved place to practise or breathe deeply and wait until the nuisance goes away voluntarily.

Before Starting Off

Before starting off let us look at other aspects of sport which may be of interest to unicyclists. These aspects, all specifically related to unicycling, are namely warming up and gymnastics, preliminary balance exercises without the unicycle and the learning of new movements.

Warming up

Sporting experience and the findings of sport psychologists speak in favour of it; warming up is an important part of athletic activity - it has an intensifying effect on all subsequent actions. (Knebel 1985, p.65). By warm-up activities we mean measures which prepare the athlete for the impending strain in a physical and psychological sense (Freiwald 1991).

Whereas less energetic conditioning by means of saunas, sun-beds and warm baths is rather ineffective in this respect and in practice plays only a minor role, an active warm-up has a number of positive effects, among which are:

- raising the capacity of the nervous system.
- reducing the risk of injury to the muscles, tendons and ligaments, in the short- and long-term.

- reducing the strain on the joints.
- compensating for lack of exercise.
- psychological well-being
  (de Marées/Mester 1982, p.69).

The range and intensity of the warm-up exercises depend on a number of factors:

Training objectives: Difficult or new exercises require intensive preparation.

Age: The time allocated to warming-up increases with age.

Time of day: More warm-up time is required in the mornings, somewhat less in the evenings.

The warm-up routine can be summarized in the following terms: "limbering up, stretching, strengthening".

Limbering up

Unicycling is well-suited for limbering up. There is a greater demand on the muscles, but it does not sap your strength. You should not attempt risky and strenuous exercises at this stage. If you are still unable to ride confidently on a unicycle you can limber up on a bicycle. 5 to 10 minutes is recommended.

Stretching

Exercises which actively or passively stretch the relevant muscle groups should follow limbering up. The principal muscle groups involved are those at the front and back of the leg and the gluteal muscles (buttocks). Light stretching should be sufficient if the subsequent practice programme contains no vigorous movements which extend the joints to the limit. This happens very rarely when unicycling - especially at the beginning.

Some examples of suitable stretching exercises have been put together based on whether they are feasible outdoors. If you practise in a hall, where you can lie on the floor, the range of possible exercises is extensively widened and improved. The arrows show the main muscle groups to be stretched. Exercising in small doses before and after training is generally sufficient for unicycling. Hold each exercise for 10-30 seconds and repeat it about 5 times.

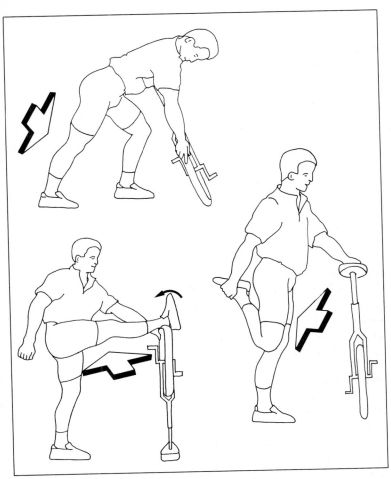

Stretching exercises

Strengthening

After stretching you can do further gymnastic strengthening exercises of the muscles. Again a unicycle is well-suited for this, for example by means of a short sprint or a hill climb and/or descent.

Warming-down

In the same way that you warm-up for the demands of athletic activity, it is sensible to warm-down afterwards to harmonize yourself psychologically and physically. This warm-down need not be too strenuous an exercise on the unicycle, it should be geared to slacken off gradually in intensity. Some stretching then follows, particularly taking into account your leg muscles which have been shortened and put under a lot of stress. The exercises for this are the same as those in the stretching period of the warm-up (details on this in Knebel 1985, Freiwald 1991).

Preliminary exercises without the unicycle

Balancing exercises and exercises for strengthening the legs without the unicycle may at first seem useful preparation but they can never replace unicycling itself; they are only of very limited value but are better than nothing.

A 'rola-bola', as jugglers describe it, is recommended as a useful exercise towards developing balance and coordination. A rola-bola consists of a wooden board (50 x 25 x 20 cm) placed on top of a cylindrical piece of tubing.

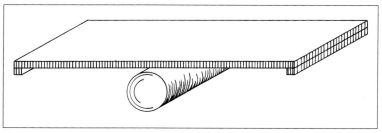

Balance can be developed using the rola-bola.

Wooden slats are attached to the underside of the board at the ends. These prevent the board from rolling off. The metal or plastic tube should be about 25 cm long with a diameter of 8-10 cm (Böhm/Born 1976, p.30).

The objective when practising with a rola-bola is to keep your balance on it as long as possible. Once you get the hang of it, which can happen quite quickly, you can perform various other moves. It becomes more difficult with the knees (half) bent. This apparatus, difficult to begin with, is good preparation for juggling on a unicycle. The exercises can be performed with the rola-bola in the long position (forwards-backwards balance) or the cross-position (sideways balance).

Some balance routines can also be performed on a bicycle, away from normal street traffic, of course, such as:

- *Riding one-handed*
- *Riding with no hands:* Sit up as quickly as possible to bring your centre of gravity over the saddle. Free-wheel with the cranks horizontal. If you can, slowly begin to pedal. The last step of the exercise is to ride a weaving pattern (slalom) by shifting your centre of gravity from side to side (Altig/Link 1985, p.51 ff).
- *Wheelie:* A challenging exercise is to ride along on just the back wheel - known as a 'wheelie'. To do this pull back hard on the handlebars and raise the front wheel up in the air. Mountain bikes with particularly low gears are good for this. When doing a wheelie on a bicycle you have to constantly maintain the balance with an interplay of rear braking and pedalling. If the front wheel falls forward towards the ground you have to pedal harder - if it rears up too much and threatens to tip you off backwards, apply the brakes. The exercise is easier if the saddle is angled sharply downwards.
- *Skate-bike:* A skate-bike is basically quite different from a unicycle. It has three wheels, a large one behind and two smaller ones next to each other at the front, though like a unicycle it has no steering mechanism. The two front wheels are similar to the rollers on a skateboard.

Riding a skate-bike is considerably easier than riding a unicycle - you simply get on and cycle off. If you can borrow such a bike, or you have one yourself, you can ride around and become accustomed to the lack of steering and the upright sitting position, which is very similar to the sitting position on a unicycle.

Skate-bike

Learning new movements

The ability to move is something which has to be learnt. No-one remembers learning how to walk, perhaps a few will remember learning how to ride a bike or to roller-skate. Something similar happens with unicycling.

Until you reach perfection you go through several stages of learning and ability:

- The beginner stage
- The advanced stage
- The expert stage

Beginner stage

The initial stages of learning are often frustrating, for even with full concentration you predominantly experience failure. After a bit of practice you begin to experience the tiniest success and you develop at some point a feel for the initial sequence of movements. With a bit more practice you can do the movements fairly roughly, but you will still make many mistakes.

Advanced stage

The sequence of movements begins to work better and it becomes increasingly possible to make corrections. The number of errors is reduced in the course of the practice sessions, though now and again things do not work out due to poor conditions or lack of concentration.

Expert stage

Only after a great deal of practice is the movement no longer a problem - you have mastered it without thinking, it is automatic and possible under the most varied conditions and distractions. It has become so automatic that your attention can be directed to other things.

Whether you are learning an easy or a difficult manoeuvre on the unicycle, you will not simply conquer it overnight; to reach the expert stage you have to feel your way slowly. To do this you first of all have to picture the movement. This picture contains current information about the movement which is summarized and stored in the brain from where it is retrievable. By reading through the descriptions of the techniques in this book and looking at the photos you can get a reasonably good idea of how to perform a particular unicycle technique. For beginners the mental picture of the movement is based on very little valuable experience and is consequently inaccurate and unclear. With an expert, however, the picture is very precise because of greater experience and more accurate impressions.

When learning the movement the picture you have of it should be improved to the point of perfection by perceptions and impressions as you perform it. The ability to take in information from what happens around you via the sensory organs and the ability to process it is fundamentally important in improving the picture you have of the movement and is consequently vital in the learning of it. These points should be clarified with an example. Very good unicyclists or circus performers often wear shoes with an extremely thin sole for unicycling. This makes sense for top riders because direct contact between foot and pedal via thin soles allows more and precise information to be taken in via changes in pressure on the sole of the foot. With this extra information they can react more quickly and more appropriately to deviations. Beginners, on the other hand, are not able to process such a flood of information about the movement of the unicycle, and much detailed information is neglected because the processing centre in the brain is overloaded with it. For this reason, and with regard to the safety aspect (when falling your feet can get caught in or on top of the unicycle), beginners should wear sturdy shoes with a rather thicker sole, though not too thick. Although information is lost with a thicker sole, information which more advanced unicyclists can use well towards controlling the movement, this need not be negative in the early stages because a beginner is simply not able to use this information.

Balance on the unicycle (desired) is ensured through specific compensatory movements of the muscles. This balance, however, is continually disrupted by the unstable balance situation and by various disturbances (uneven floor, movement of own body). The unicyclist constantly takes in information about the momentary position of the body and the unicycle (actual) via the different sensory organs. This information is:

— heard through the sound of the tyre,
— observed in terms of rocking and swaying,
— felt via pressure between the foot and the pedal and the backside and the saddle,
— noted via linear and tension changes in the muscles and
— established through changes in balance.

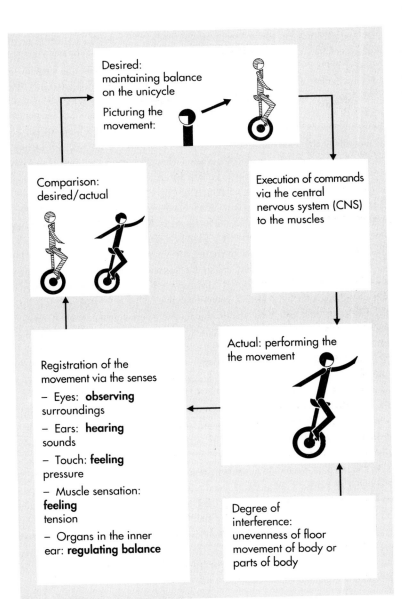

Desired:
maintaining balance
on the unicycle

Picturing the
movement:

Comparison:
desired/actual

Execution of commands
via the central
nervous system (CNS)
to the muscles

Registration of the
movement via the senses

– Eyes: **observing**
surroundings

– Ears: **hearing**
sounds

– Touch: **feeling**
pressure

– Muscle sensation:
feeling
tension

– Organs in the inner
ear: **regulating balance**

Actual: performing the
the movement

Degree of
interference:
unevenness of floor
movement of body or
parts of body

Regulating balance on the unicycle

The registration of the movement (actual) is conveyed to the central nervous system (CNS) and compared with the picture you have of the movement, i.e. the plan of maintaining balance on the unicycle (desired). By establishing differences between the desired and the actual, orders are passed on by the CNS for the muscles to make corrections.

In the learning process the actual and the desired should be brought closer until the two match. Correcting errors plays an important role in the process. In many sporting activities a coach is engaged to correct errors. Very few unicyclists will have a coach, but this is not too important because the role of coach in correcting errors is largely carried out by the unicycle itself. Bad errors of execution are punished immediately by the unicycle - it falls over. As both a piece of sporting apparatus and as a coach the unicycle is a teaching machine.

Perhaps you can imagine learning the movements this way: Like grooves on a record, each practice session leaves tracks in your mechanical memory. With just a little practice these grooves are only very superficially engrained. If you want to play everything back you have to concentrate extremely hard, but even with great effort the grooves cannot be exactly located. The exercise is perhaps recognizable in structure, but it is unclear and fragmented. Intensive practice leaves behind deep grooves carved out in exact detail and instantly retraceable. The playing back of the movements you have stored occurs smoothly and without great effort.

Every time you practise, traces are left behind in the movement memory. Even if you register no discernible success after a period of practising, it is worth remembering: Practice was not recommended without good reason!

Try to practise unicycling techniques with both the left and the right side of the body. Certainly if you practise and learn on just one side the weaker side will benefit to some extent because the stronger side has laid the foundations for learning. However, if you want to perform techniques on both sides (symmetricalisation), you should also work on the weaker side of the body. This not only improves your ability on the weaker side but leads to an improvement on the dominant side as well.

When nothing goes right

There are stages in the learning process when you are in despair - nothing is going right. You are not progressing, and tricks which you thought you had mastered you can no longer do at all. Instead of getting better, things threaten to get worse with further practice.

Such stages emerge in almost every long-term planned learning process. They are irritating, but quite common. Particularly when you are tired you find your coordination, based on maximum concentration, breaks down easily. The best remedy is to take a short break from practice. This break is used to settle yourself and to distract your mind before resuming the exercise with renewed concentration. Normally just a few minutes are sufficient.

If a brief rest does not help, it is advisable to take a complete break from practising. This break is used to analyse the situation. Overworking can often lead to stagnation. If you get fed up with unicycling, you would be well advised to put it to one side for a while and continue later with new spirit.

Too much impatience can also lead to errors. For example, bunny-hopping on the unicycle is fun, but you will learn it more easily if you have prepared for it beforehand by perfecting some basic techniques. So that you do not encourage failure you would do well to wait until the time is right to practise. Gross neglect of individual learning steps usually brings bad results.

Impatience can also put you under pressure. If you have made up your mind unconditionally to learn a technique in one day, and not to stop until you have done it, you put yourself under unnecessary pressure to succeed. Setting practice targets for yourself is quite sensible, but it is wrong to try to achieve your set goals with force. If you feel that despite your best efforts that it is just not happening today, end the session and the stress. Things usually go better the next day.

How long is the learning process?

"Riding a unicycle is easy and can be quickly learned" (Böhm/Born 1976, p. 263). This is a sentence from a textbook on trick-cycling. But it is not quite so simple if you are not a trick-cyclist and are unlikely to be one.

Frustration awaits the beginner, but the seemingly futile attempts of the first half hour on the unicycle are quickly forgotten. The speed at which you learn depends on a number of factors. Firstly, of course, much depends on how long you practise; the more you practise, the more you learn. How much can you learn, though, within a given practice session? In five hours of practice, for example, the amount learned can differ considerably from person to person. It depends on motivation, on the practice conditions, on the learning methods employed, on your experiences of the motion involved, and on age.

Motivation
Broadly speaking, motivation is the impetus for action. Such impetus can be extremely strong and occur frequently, at other times it can be weak and occur only occasionally. Having fun with your unicycling may be the best motivation, but in the long-term you will only have fun if you register some success. The speed at which the successful learn can increase further with this 'booster' effect.

Learning and practice conditions
Favourable conditions for learning and practice are large spaces free of disturbance, level ground and somewhere to support yourself. Whichever of the teaching methods described in this book lead to maximum success differs for each individual, but a stimulating environment among those of like mind can have a positive effect on how successfully you learn.

Teaching methods
When learning you can proceed differently and apply various strategies. If you proceed with the methods described as follows (from page 50) and tackle the practice exercises, then a specific search for the correct methods will soon prove successful.

If you try to learn by the 'trial and error' method, i.e. without instruction, success will come to you rather more hesitantly and by chance. However, applying the undisputed best methods brings the biggest success: "The best teaching method is: Rousing a passion for something" (Benesch 1987, p. 155)

Experience of related movements

People who have already learnt many different movements and committed them automatically to memory will learn new ones more quickly. This is true particularly for movements already perfected from related sports with an emphasis on coordination, and especially on maintaining balance.

Age

The development of your coordination, and in this respect particularly the development of balance, plays an important part in the speed at which you learn. Such capabilities develop continually from childhood to puberty. At the beginning of puberty the development of balance slows or continues only negligibly. As you get older it takes longer to learn things since the practice of absorbing and processing information deteriorates. To become a brilliant unicyclist you really have to start at a very young age.

A decisive factor for learning quickly, however, is a combination of all the above-mentioned factors (motivation, conditions, teaching methods, experience of the movement and age). If you are lacking in one area, you can compensate for it in others. Strong motivation in particular can be most effective. So although, for example, an advanced age is not particularly ideal for developing coordination quickly, a desire to practise and a sense of fun with your unicycling can balance this out. If you maximise all the factors described above you can learn to unicycle in one day (riding forwards 25 metres without falling off). If you practise for about 45 minutes every day, then as a good mean average you should be able to ride forwards 25 metres fairly competently within about a week. An easy exercise, such as riding forwards, requires a relatively short learning time. The more difficult and demanding the exercises are, the longer it takes to learn them.

Basic Techniques
of Unicycle Riding

"Even a journey of 1000 miles
begins with the first step."
(Eastern wisdom)

Starting off

Crucial to the basic techniques of unicycle riding is a coordinated interaction of both legs. Either the right or the left leg can take on the more important role depending on the position of the pedal. For example, a mounting technique can be performed by shifting the weight onto the right leg, but the same mounting technique is equally possible using the other side of your body, i.e. shifting the weight onto the left leg.

The instructions for performing the exercises are given each time for one side only (usually the right). To begin with, practise with your stronger leg. This way you will get successful results earlier and the movement perfected on one side gives you the confidence and the idea of the movement for learning the same technique on your weaker side. The objective is to master the basic technique on both sides. Falling off or even just dismounting unintentionally is not failure; rather it is proof that the learning process is in full swing.

Learning to ride:
The key to having fun on the unicycle

The first step in learning to ride a unicycle is getting someone to help you mount and help you keep your balance during your first attempts. What sort of assistance you can call upon will vary from person to person. Not everyone will be able to get two people to help them mount and ride the unicycle and only very few people will have access at the beginning to a gym or hall. Since, therefore, the circumstances under which people learn may differ, various methods are described to show how you to ride a unicycle. Each method described leads to the same objective, regardless of whether you proceed with just one of them or whether you combine several by practising some of the time alone, some of the time with one person to help you, and at other times with two.

Whichever method you choose, however, they all have one thing in common; in the early stages the power relationship between you and the unicycle is quite clear - it controls you. It will take a little while to change this relationship in your favour.

Balance exercises

Balance exercises can be the very first step to unicycling. Through balance exercises you gain your first experiences on the unicycle. For this you require a practice space with a very stable support which you can hold on to with both hands, like a doorway or a post. Hold on to the support, climb up on the unicycle and try to stay on it. If after a while you feel fairly confident, move back and forth a few centimetres. This way you learn how the unicycle reacts to your movements.

Learning with help

It is possible to tip over in any direction on a unicycle, which broadly speaking means forwards, backwards and sideways. Compare this to a bicycle. On a bicycle you can fall over to the sides but not generally forwards or backwards. The particular problem with unicycling, therefore, is the forwards-backwards balance. The problem of balancing sideways can be disregarded in the early learning stages by getting support from the sides. This way you can concentrate completely on the unfamiliar forwards-backwards balance.

Mounting with two helpers and a wedge under the wheel

The easiest way to begin is the mount with a wedge behind the wheel. To do this, place the wheel against a kerb or something similar to act as a brake. Stand behind the unicycle and bring the cranks into a horizontal position, the right one nearest to you. With the saddle between your legs and your left foot on the ground, place your right foot on the right pedal. Your assistants stand one either side of you - you can hold on to their shoulders or they can hold onto your arms. Now push off from the floor with the left foot and place it on the left pedal (photos p.53 top). The unicycle is prevented from rolling in 3 of the 4 directions by the two helpers and the 'wedge'. Once you are supported, with cranks horizontal, you can then venture forth.

Mounting the unicycle with two helpers and a wedge under the wheel

Mounting with two helpers and a free wheel

The correct starting position for this mount is with the saddle between your legs, your left foot on the ground and your right foot on the right pedal. The frame of the unicycle is inclined towards you. The right crank should be angled between you and the ground. Hold onto to your helpers, who are positioned either side of you. Now push up from the floor with your left leg.

Mounting the unicycle with two helpers and no wedge

This will apply pressure on the right pedal, pushing it down into its lowest position. At the same time the unicycle moves into the upright position and you are lifted up onto the saddle. The helpers must provide good support during this unstable stage. If you manage to get on, bring the cranks into the horizontal position and away you go.

Learning with two helpers

Start off as follows: With the cranks horizontal, cycle forwards a half-turn of the wheel until the cranks are into the next horizontal position. Pause. Do another half-turn, pause, go on, pause etc. Your helpers walk and stop at the same pace.

It is easier at the beginning to pedal from a horizontal crank postion. So that you do not get stuck with the cranks completely vertical, and therefore forcing you to step off the unicycle, be constantly aware that the cranks should always be brought to rest in the horizontal position. As you go along, try to bring most of your body weight onto the saddle.

There are a number of ways in which your assistants can support you. Many beginners feel it is helpful to hold on to the shoulders of the helpers, thereby regulating the pressure themselves. By experimenting with other possibilities and ways of holding on, you will discover the type of support which suits you best.

Learning with two helpers

If moving forwards a half-turn at a time, as described above, goes well, you can then try it with one complete revolution of the wheel. So, with the cranks horizontal, pedal one complete turn, pause with the pedals once more in the horizontal position, do another complete turn, pause etc. If you feel fairly confident with this exercise pedal more continuously and pause less often.

Learning with one helper

When you can ride a bit more steadily, you can dispense with one of the helpers. The remaining one now supports you alternately from the right side and the left. Changing over is important. It makes you work both sides of the body and stops you from leaning to one side when you try it alone later. Support can also be given by a competent unicyclist riding alongside you.

Learning with one helper

Starting to ride alone

As you get better you will fall off less often and feel confident enough to ride without any support, if only for a few brief moments. At this stage it is helpful when going forwards to keep your balance by holding your arms out to the sides. When riding with just a little help you will at some point manage a few metres on your own, experiencing for the first time the true feeling of unicycling; this is the decisive breakthrough! Your first few metres confirm that you are now in the process of mastering the unicycle and not the other way around, as at the beginning.

Dismounting

At this stage you have probably been able to cycle for just a short while and your attempts have ended abruptly with a fairly unexpected loss of balance. That should now change. From now on you should try to end every successful trip with a controlled dismount in which you keep hold of the unicycle. There are two ways to do this; either stepping off behind the unicycle or in front of it.

To prepare for a dismount behind the unicycle you must firstly reduce your speed a little. Pedal slowly and evenly, and incline your upper body backwards (photo above left). In this position the unicycle tends to roll forwards. Take hold of the front of the saddle with one hand, take your feet off the pedals one after the other and stand up (photo below left).

Dismounting backwards

Dismounting forwards

For a frontal dismount, slow down and simply stop pedalling. Keep your body upright and the saddle will incline forwards with you (photo above left). Grab the saddle behind you with one hand, then take the feet off the pedals one after the other and stand up (photo above right).

The role of the helper

After a while it becomes boring being the helper while others do the learning. The best solution is for the rider and the helper to exchange roles from time to time. In this way the two can remain fully involved and can, when things are not going so well, console and encourage each other. The quality demanded most from the helper (and the rider too) is patience.

The risks of injury to the helpers are thankfully low. In their supporting role they are more in danger from the wild arm movements of the rider than the falling unicycle, which usually rolls forwards or backwards away from the helpers standing to the left and right. However, they can receive scratches or a box round the ears from these wild arm movements when the rider reaches out for help. Some unicyclists cling with considerable tenacity to the arms, shoulders, head, hair or clothes of the people supporting them. This usually happens during the learning stages as people try to stay on the unicycle, and occasionally try to pedal without support. It is best if the helpers wear tough, elasticated clothing which can endure a severe tugging.

Picking up the unicycle

If the unicycle falls to the floor, there is a simple way of picking it up without bending down and damaging your back. Hook your foot under the seat-post, near the top, and raise your leg so that you can reach the unicycle with your hand.

Picking up the unicycle

Learning to ride by yourself

If for some reason you are unable to practise with others, or you do not want to, you can learn on your own just as effectively. What you need is a support to hold onto as you sit on the saddle. Depending on your practice space, this can be a doorway, a post, a fence or a wall etc. It should be something which you can both reach for, and let go of, as you move along.

Firstly you have to get on the unicycle with the help of your chosen support. To do this stand behind the unicycle with the frame inclined towards you and place the saddle between your legs. Your left foot is on the ground, your right on the right pedal. The right crank is angled towards you and the ground. Hold onto the support with both hands (later just one). Now push up off the ground with your left foot. This applies pressure to the right pedal which is forced into its lowest position. The unicycle moves into the upright position and you with it. Once up, try to bring the cranks into a horizontal position.

A good spot for learning by yourself: here you can support yourself from both sides.

Learning by yourself: support yourself with both hands to begin with

... then with just the one.

From this position cycle forwards a half-turn until the cranks are once more in a horizontal position. Pause briefly. Go forwards again, pause, go forwards etc. As you do so move your hands along the support which you are using. Make sure that you support yourself alternately from the right side and from the left. If, for example, you support yourself from the left side only, you will find when trying it later without support that you veer to the left all the time.

You will have to spend some time on this exercise (a few hours) until you can cover a few metres on your own. As you feel more and more confident, reduce your reliance on the support. The feeling of being able to ride freely is the breakthrough in unicycling.

After a bit of practice, and regardless of which method you learn by, you will soon be able to ride 20 metres or more without support and fairly confidently. This is the start of endless fun on your unicycle.

Riding the Unicycle

Practice and coaching tips

After you have negotiated the difficult first hurdle, learning to ride the unicycle, the next step is to consolidate and develop your ability under different conditions. You must practise regularly and often if you want to become a really good unicyclist. Some tips may help you to avoid making unnecessary mistakes as you practise and consequently help you to reach your targets more quickly.

- Every time you practise set yourself specific and realistic goals. This helps you to concentrate and therefore be more effective.
- Make a note of your progress.
- Set yourself intermediate goals, for example: "In two weeks I want to be able to ride for ten minutes without dismounting" or "At the end of this month I want to be able to mount the unicycle without help."
- Make the most of falling off! Falls and dismounts give you the opportunity to practise different mounting techniques. If you can only do one type of mount, try it with the right and the left leg alternately.
- Consider the mental side of unicycling. Talk about your practice sessions and your successes (but not to the extent that you drive people crazy).

- Practise new techniques or try to successfully complete new practice exercises. You should practise new tricks about 15 minutes after the beginning of a session. The time prior to that should incorporate a warm-up, some stretching exercises (if necessary) and a short recap of what you have already learned.
- Try not to practise new techniques after very strenuous physical activity. There is no point in working on technique when you are tired.
- Practise tricks with both the left and the right side of the body, and with the left and right leg.
- Plan your practice session so that you learn new techniques as well as repeating and perfecting those you have already learnt.
- Positively avoid moving your hands and arms into "hopeless" positions. In other words do not put your hands in your pockets as you ride along or try to pull a jumper over your head.
- Do not unicycle with fragile or dangerous objects. You can do a lot with your free hands when unicycling, but do not drink from a glass bottle or spread bread with a knife.
- Unicycling with a Walkman can be both good and bad. On the one hand the music can be stimulating and the rhythm may be helpful to practise to. On the other hand you will not hear any (warning-) signals from the environment around you.
- Gradually try to complete as many different practice exercises as possible. These practice exercises are highlighted in the following text in small boxes. It is not necessary to have learned each exercise completely before moving on to the next one. Indeed in the course of time you should attempt as many practice exercises as possible, for you can only come back to some of them when you have improved and become more confident on the unicycle. Make a note of the exercises you have done to gain an overall view of your progress. For some of them write down how and what you achieved, for example "rode one mile without dismounting" or "rode a stretch between two lamp-posts in 17 seconds" or "completed 3 free-mounts within 5 minutes".

Riding with vision

Certainly the slightest loss of concentration on the unicycle at the beginning can lead to difficulties. Therefore, you should practise observing your surroundings as you go along.

Count some prominent objects as you go along, like trees, fence-posts, people, dogs etc.
When unicycling in the open air study the countryside in detail.
Try looking at your watch as you ride along.
Extend your field of vision by looking to the right and left.
Try looking behind you as you ride along.

Covering distances

With these exercises your pedalling becomes more regular and economical and your technique becomes sounder.

Cycle several miles non-stop.
Try to improve your time over a fixed stretch or to reduce the number of unintentional dismounts.
Cycle for specific periods of time, like 5, 10, 15 or 30 minutes.

In some places you may have to dismount where there is nothing to hold onto. It is therefore important to learn to mount the unicycle without any form of support.

Mounting without help

Mounting without help is best learnt after you have gained a little confidence on the unicycle:
Standing behind the unicycle, incline the frame towards you and place the saddle between your legs. Hold the saddle with one hand to start off with, later you can perform the mount without the use of your hands. The right crank points towards you, angled to the floor. Your left foot is on the ground and your right foot is on the right pedal. Now push up from the floor with your left leg. This applies pressure to the right pedal, which is forced down into its lowest position. This action lifts you upwards. The real problem of balance begins now, firstly because you no longer have contact with the floor and secondly because your left foot must be placed as quickly as possible on the left pedal.

Free-mount from behind the unicycle

If you have done this successfully, counteract the backward movement of the pedals initiated when you mounted the unicycle by braking with both feet and set off forwards.

One of the main problems with this mount is the shift in body weight. In order to mount the unicycle you must apply pressure to the right pedal, but if you apply too much, for too long, the right pedal gets 'marooned' in its lowest position and the mount will fail. Try to bring your body weight quickly onto the saddle and take the weight off the right pedal.

What sounds simple and obvious in explanation is in practice not quite so simple at first. You will need a number of attempts before you master the free-mount.

Find a quiet and unobserved place and practise the free-mount.
Voluntarily dismount the unicycle after a minute at the most and free-mount again.
Do as many free-mounts as possible within 3 minutes.
Do as many free-mounts as possible within 3 minutes, alternating between the left and the right leg.

Changing direction, Making turns

At first your changes of direction will be very laborious and jerky. It will take a while before you can do small turns and ride in circles. It is slightly easier if you hold your arms up to the side, developing your shoulder muscles at the same time.

To begin making a turn, incline your body gently in the direction in which the turn is to be made. This long turning movement of the upper body is then transferred via the hips and backside to the unicycle.

Make a big turn of 90°.
Make a big turn of 180°.
Ride in a large circle.
Gradually reduce the radius of the turn in each case.
Practise turns and circles to the right and to the left.

Slalom courses and figures

Line up some small stones at a distance of several metres from each other. Use them as a slalom course to ride around. Gradually reduce the distance between the stones.
Arrange more difficult slalom courses.
Time how long it takes to complete a slalom course. Try to improve your time.

Perform a figure-of-eight. Try to reduce the size of it during the practice session.

Try to 'draw' large letters, like a 'P' or an 'S' for example.

Follow closely behind somebody on a bike as they make slow turns.

Try to follow exactly behind another unicyclist at a distance of about 3 metres.

Slalom riding

Changing speed

There are limitations to how fast you can ride a unicycle. These limitations are determined by the speed at which you can move your legs and by centrifugal force. The maximum speed on a unicycle is reached when you are pedalling so fast that your feet fly off the pedals. When riding extremely quickly you must, therefore, pedal at a speed at which you are able to keep your feet flat on the pedals. Easy to say, though in practice not quite so simple to achieve.

It is just as difficult turning your unicycle into a snail as it is into a racehorse. When cycling extremely slowly you should avoid large sideways movements. Practise within lateral boundaries, such as chalk lines, narrow paths etc.

Ride along a predetermined stretch as quickly as possible.
Try to ride along a predetermined stretch as slowly as possible.
Ride along, alternating between 10 quick revolutions of the cranks and 10 slow ones. Gradually reduce this number until you reach a point where you are doing one quick and one slow revolution.

Unicycling in public:
Testing your proficiency

As we know, unicycling is not generally permitted on roads. Strictly speaking this rule also applies to cycle tracks and footpaths, though there is no obvious reason why this should not be permitted if you can ride competently enough.

Before you join in with other cyclists and pedestrians on these public thoroughfares you would do well to give yourself a little proficiency test beforehand in riding, mounting and dismounting the unicycle, and in avoiding other road users. The following test may be useful:

- ☐ Attempt 10 free-mounts, one after the other. At least 9 of them must be successful.
- ☐ Cycle continuously for 10 minutes. You may dismount twice at the most, on each occasion holding on to the unicycle.
- ☐ Mark out a slalom course with 6 small stones or other objects at a distance of around 3 metres (paces) from each other. Negotiate the course 10 times. At least 9 of the attempts should be faultless.
- ☐ Cycle towards an obstacle and dismount about 3 metres in front of it. Do this 20 times, alternating between a frontal dismount and one to the rear, holding onto the unicycle each time. All 20 attempts should be successful.

If you did not pass the test it is better to keep practising away from movable objects. If you passed the test you can ride competently enough to present no danger to yourself or others, though remember that applies only to footpaths and cycle tracks. In no way does passing this test give you the right to unicycle on the roads.

Combinations with other movements

Up to this point your arms have probably been outstretched to the side as you cycle along, making inelegant jerky movements to maintain your balance. You should now learn to control your arms more, but at this stage in your learning this could be a disruptive factor which may lead initially to a somewhat unstable feeling when riding.

By controlling your arm movements you learn to move your upper body purposefully and independently from the pedalling. This will improve your riding style and in the long-term you will be able to hold your arms in a loose and relaxed fashion.

Controlled and consciously directed arm movements enable you to juggle on the unicycle. Exercises which work towards a combination of unicycle and juggling are marked with a (J).

Clap your hands as you ride along.
Fold your arms in front of your body.
Clasp your hands behind your neck or behind your back.
Make small or large circles with your arms as you ride along.
Ride with your hands on your knees.
Try to shift the position of your feet on the pedals as you go along.
Try to put as much of your body weight as possible on the saddle and only a little on the pedals.
Shift as much of your body weight as possible onto the pedals so that hardly any weight is on the saddle.

Extend both legs each time the cranks are horizontal and stand up briefly.
Touch your shoes as you go along.
(J) Throw a ball from one hand to the other.
(J) Try to exchange two balls with throws at head height (see page 147).
(J) If you can juggle three balls quite well try to do it on the unicycle as you go along (difficult exercise).

Riding up and downhill

The steepness of slope you attempt depends not only on your ability, but also on the size of the wheel. The larger the wheel, the more difficult it is because you have to pedal harder. When descending you practise your braking. Both exercises develop the leg muscles.

You brake when descending by applying counter pressure with your legs against the rising pedal pushing against your sole and slowing you down. To support this braking motion sit less heavily on the saddle and move your body weight onto the braking pedal.

Cycle down steep slopes.
Cycle up gradients.
Cycle up and down slopes both in a straight line and in zigzags.

Riding over small obstacles

It is easier to ride down a kerb than to ride up one. There is a limit to the height of obstacles over which you can unicycle; a height of between 10 to 15 cm or more is not easy to negotiate.

Descending such heights, on the other hand, causes no insurmountable difficulties. In riding over obstacles it will help you to shift your body weight from the saddle onto both pedals equally and to stand up slightly.

Practise negotiating small kerbs or similar obstacles of a few centimetres in height (descending and ascending). Do not approach too slowly.

Ride down kerbs or similar obstacles. Try to gradually increase the height of the obstacles to be negotiated.

Unicycling cross-country

Cross-country unicycle trips are only justified if you can be certain that they are still environmentally friendly.

Cycle on woodland paths or other unsurfaced paths.

Cycle over a patch of grass. Since the grass will undergo enough damage simply by riding forwards evenly, it should not be ruined further by changing direction and ploughing up the ground with the tyre.

Style of riding

All well executed tricks give the observer the impression that they are performed in an easy and relaxed way and without too much exertion. The more casual and relaxed the unicyclist appears, the better the riding style.

Sit upright in the saddle with your head held straight, as though a string is attached to it like a puppet. Look directly forwards. Your arms can hang loosely next to your body or you can link your hands behind your back. With relaxed features, you can give the impression that you are enjoying yourself. The aim of a good riding style is the ability to ride in a straight line without swerving. The jerky riding style, almost inevitable at first, disappears as you improve. Your pedalling should then become smooth and even without hesitant awkward pauses.

Cycle with your back to the sun and test your riding style by observing your shadow on a wall or the ground.

Be photographed or filmed as you cycle and use the pictures to assess your technique.

Turning sharply

Changing direction on the unicycle need no longer be a problem at this stage. You have already practised making gentle turns, now you should learn to make particularly sharp ones, i.e. turns which are as tight as possible and are made in a very small space. Whereas you need several revolutions of the cranks for making large turns, sharp turns should be made with just one firm downward push on the pedal.

The unicycle is turned immediately to the left by pushing down hard on the left pedal. The upper body is already pointing in the desired direction.

You can turn so tightly that it appears as if you are turning on the spot.

Cycle forwards normally and reduce your speed so that the unicycle almost comes to a halt. If you are making a left turn, the left pedal should be in the forwards horizontal position. Hold both arms out to the sides and twist your upper body to the left. At this stage your upper body is turned towards the desired direction of travel, whilst the lower body still points in the original direction. A forceful downward push on the left pedal causes your lower body to twist in the direction in which your upper body is already turned, and in this way you make your sharp left turn. To begin with, try to make 90° turns to the left and to the right. After a little practice you will be able to make 180° turns. Since the turns are always made with the wheel in the same position, this exercise can lead to rapid wear of the tyre.

Make a sharp 45° turn.
Make a sharp 90° turn.
Make a sharp 180° turn.
Practise turns to the left and right.

Riding Backwards

Riding backwards on a unicycle is not only a challenge, it is also a great deal of fun. As a basic skill it is an important step towards learning more difficult and technical tricks. If you want to do more on a unicycle than cycle to the post box every now and again, you should learn to ride backwards.

Unfortunately, even if you are fairly competent when riding forwards, you become a complete beginner again when it comes to learning to ride backwards. Even riding a few metres may take a little bit longer than the time it took learning to ride forwards, but don't worry, if you can ride forwards you have already shown considerable persistence and skill and you will also master this new technique.

Technically speaking, your first attempts to ride backwards are a new start. You can proceed methodically from the beginning as you did when learning to ride forwards, but the difference is that new difficulties arise due to the new direction of motion. The problem of turning your head and looking behind you represents a new challenge. The learning procedure, with and without help, is similar to that of learning to ride forwards.

Riding backwards

Learning to ride backwards with help

As with riding forwards, the main difficulty when going backwards is maintaining the forwards-backwards balance. So that you focus your full concentration on this, the problem of sideways balance can be eliminated in the early stages by getting someone to help you.

Riding backwards with two helpers

Either mount the unicycle between the two helpers or ride slowly up between them with your arms outstretched and come to a halt, holding onto them firmly. Bring the cranks into the horizontal position and pedal backwards half a revolution of the wheel. After this half-turn the pedals should again be in the horizontal position. Continue practising like this; a half-turn, pause, a half-turn, pause etc. As you pedal backwards your helpers, facing the opposite direction, walk forwards with you. When you begin to feel comfortable with this exercise, you can firstly try one complete revolution of the cranks, then later several revolutions one after the other. As your confidence grows you will rely less and less on your helpers until you can travel the first few metres alone.

Riding backwards with two helpers

Riding backwards with one helper

You can also learn to ride backwards with just one person to help you. The method corresponds to that of starting off with two helpers, though it may be more demanding because the problem of sideways balance is only resolved by support from one side. So that you do not keel over later due to continual support from one particular side, the person assisting you should alternate between the left and the right sides.

Riding backwards with one helper

Learning to ride backwards by yourself

A practice space with something to hold onto is essential. After mounting the unicycle bring the cranks into the horizontal position. From this position pedal backwards half a revolution of the wheel until the cranks are once again horizontal. Pause briefly. Do a half-turn again, pause, continue on etc. As you do so, move your hands along whatever it is you have chosen to support yourself. After a little while you should be able to cycle backwards one complete revolution of the cranks, and later several one after the other. When you have practised this exercise long enough (several hours) you will want, at some point, to try to cycle a few revolutions without holding on to your support. Initially this will feel very unsteady and last only a few metres. Do not fear; you would be most unlucky to end up on your back like a beetle, for when falling backwards you usually end up on your feet.

Ideal conditions for learning to ride backwards: Support from both sides

Exercises for riding backwards

A few practice exercises should ensure that you master riding backwards with more confidence and versatility. The degree of difficulty increases with each exercise.

Cycle backwards slowly, then quickly, then slowly again.
Cover a series of long stretches one after the other.
Ride backwards looking over your left and right shoulder alternately.
Ride backwards with your hands clasped in front of your body.
Ride in zigzags.
Make a large turn to the left, then one to the right.
Ride in large circles to the right and then to the left. Do the same again making the circles smaller.
Ride backwards with your arms folded.
(J) Try to ride backwards throwing a small ball from one hand to the other.
(J) Try to ride backwards exchanging two balls with a throw at about head height (see page 147).
Ride backwards in a figure-of-eight. (J) Try to ride backwards while juggling three balls (very difficult).

When juggling and riding backwards you not only have to deal with the problems of co-ordination but also that of being unable to see where you are going. You have to look back in the direction in which you are going, and forward at the juggling balls. Make sure you practise where there is a lot of space to avoid crashing into obstacles.

Riding forwards-backwards

When you have mastered riding forwards and backwards individually you can combine both skills with each other. One way to do this is to twist round 180° as you cycle forwards and immediately continue in the same direction, but riding backwards. Here the main difficulty is doing a smooth enough half-turn which enables you to continue on your journey. You should reduce speed considerably when learning this technique in order to perform the half-turn correctly.

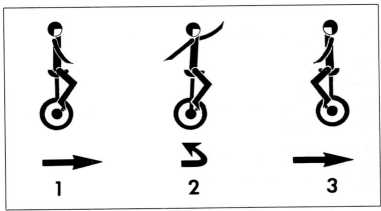

Begin the approach (1), make a quick half-turn (2) and continue backwards in the same direction (3).

Do the exercise described above with both a left and a right half-turn.

Ride backwards on the unicycle, do a quick half-turn and continue riding forwards.

Another possible combination of forwards-backwards riding is to cycle forwards, reduce speed, incline your upper body backwards just before coming to a halt and brake by applying pressure with your foot to the pedal which is on the rise. You and the unicycle consequently come to a halt, though your body is inclined backwards (photo above left). Now pedal backwards so that you do not fall off the unicycle. After a few metres riding backwards reduce speed and incline the upper body slightly forwards, just before you come to a halt (photo below left). This position makes it easier to set off forwards again.

Brake by leaning backwards and forwards respectively. To avoid falling off, pedal quickly in the direction in which your body is inclined.

Although the exercise described above sounds relatively uncomplicated, in practice it is of course not so simple at all. The main difficulty is the timing and application of the correct amount of pressure to the rising pedal. Initially, the moment at which you lean forwards or backwards, and how far you do it, is a problem. But with two things going for you, namely a feeling for the movement and persistence, you should manage to do this exercise.

Between two markers, first ride forwards and then ride backwards.

Try to cycle in as small a space as possible, starting off in a larger area and reducing it down to one about one square metre. The borders of the smaller target area can be marked out with small stones. This exercise is easier with a smaller wheel.

Hovering

Hovering is the motion by which you ride forwards and backwards on the spot with no more than a half-turn of the cranks to maintain your balance. It is a basic element of unicycling. When you master it, you will be able to take a breather when you are out riding or practising without having to dismount. You will also be able to ride in the tiniest spaces, for example on a stage.

As with previous exercises, you learn to hover by holding on to something. The foot on the pedal in the lowest position plays the predominant role in the hovering motion. Each time this foot moves forwards and backwards it should, at the right moment, execute a well-measured braking movement. The impetus in the new direction is achieved more or less equally by both feet.

The pedals only move between the white dots as you hover (photos right). As with a pendulum, the swing is greatest at the bottom, with the wheel moving to and fro acting almost like the end of the pendulum. Your head is the suspension point of the pendulum and remains still and upright.

At first you will probably wave your arms about a little. As you begin to feel more steady this flailing of the arms will gradually stop. Since you will be mounting and dismounting quite frequently when you are learning to hover, you can practise different mounting techniques at the same time (see page 64 and pages 92-104).

Hovering: One foot (here the right) moves the pedal through the lower half of the wheel. The other foot (the left) moves the pedal through the upper half.

Hovering exercises

Hold onto a suitable support as you learn to hover. Gradually try to reduce your dependence on the support.
Hover to musical rhythms of varying tempos. The object of this exercise is to hover exactly to the beat of the music.
Hover with clasped hands.
Hover with folded arms.
Hover for 3, 5, 10 minutes without a break and without dismounting.
(J)   Throw a small ball from one hand to the other while hovering.
(J)   While hovering try to exchange two balls from hand to hand with throws about head height.
(J)   Juggle 3 balls while hovering.
While hovering move the unicycle several metres to the left and then to the right.
While hovering turn the unicycle to the right and to the left.
Try reading a paper as you hover.
Try to gradually reduce the pedal motion so that you briefly become motionless.
Try hovering with your eyes closed and concentrate completely on the movement (difficult).

Riding confidently both forwards and backwards, turning, free-mounting and hovering, as well as numerous possible combinations of these skills, form the basis of unicycling. In other words - that was the compulsory unicycling programme. Everything which follows this is optional.

Advanced Techniques of Unicycle Riding

The transition from beginner to advanced unicyclist, and finally to expert, occurs in this book by simply turning the pages over one after the other, but in reality it is a slow process. In turning over the pages there is also no deviation from the basic techniques of riding a unicycle. Perhaps some advanced techniques will cause you less difficulty than one or two of the techniques classified as basic, or one or two of the practice exercises specified. It may well be that you are already practising advanced tricks without having mastered all the basic ones completely, or without having completed all the practice exercises for these tricks. As an advanced unicyclist practise the basic techniques again and again and return to those exercises which you have not yet completed. Beginner, Advanced and Expert are terms which cannot be neatly divided. Transition from beginner to expert takes place at particular junctures sometimes quickly, sometimes slowly, at times turbulently, at times calmly, at times absorbed quickly, sometimes slowly, but always consistently in one direction.

Practice -
Setting priorities

If you have learnt the basic techniques to the point where you are quite good on the unicycle, the direction you now take depends on your own individual interest and the areas into which you will now move. There are three areas of focus which can influence further practice:

The first area is leisure cycling. If you just want to unwind, to practise now and again and ride about occasionally, then fun and spontaneity should be the top priority. Plan your practice sessions with enjoyment in mind, and vary them each time by applying the same principle. Suitable exercises are therefore those which appeal to you and which are fun.

The second area is sport cycling. Here strength and conditioning are the most important aspects. You can time yourself on the unicycle and establish (individual) records. Sport cyclists can practise pedalling evenly on a unicycle with a 1:1 gear ratio. If you unicycle in addition to your main sport, to accompany your training or as a regenerative measure, you should seek out exercises with the unicycle which correspond in some way to the demands of your principal sport. For strengthening the legs you can choose specific exercises, like riding with the saddle in front or behind the body. The main emphasis will lie with techniques covering a large area (riding forwards, backwards, with one leg, not sitting on the saddle) and less on hovering. With sport cycling your practice sessions will be directed towards specific objectives and carried out systematically.

The third area is performance unicycling. This serves either to satisfy the standards you set yourself or to show off your tricks to the public. The practice sessions here aim mostly at building up the number of tricks to show off, with the emphasis on techniques which are impressive to the public, like bunny-hopping, pirouettes and wheel-walking. You can also combine unicycling with other activities, like rope-skipping or juggling. With performance riding, hovering in all its forms and in combination with other activities is a particularly important part of the practice sessions. Practise specific exercises and repeat them until you can do them competently.

The division into three central areas is not relevant to each and every unicyclist, for some people do not want to be categorized as such. The three areas are not sharply demarcated and there are smooth overlaps. If your unicycling priorities are different, or if indeed if you do not have any, here are some tips for further practice:

Even top athletes from other spheres have likes and dislikes among the techniques of their sport. With unicycling it is no different. If you tackle the advanced techniques you will find some of them are to your liking, others less so. You may decide that bunny-hopping on the unicycle is not particularly to your liking - many others have felt the same. Others, however, may be quite enthusiastic about it and hardly do anything else on their unicycle. Therefore, try out as many techniques as possible until you can do them reasonably well, and decide which ones you enjoy most. When you get an overall view, follow the techniques which appeal to you and for which you show some talent. You will develop your own unicycling style by practising certain techniques intensively and often, and because each person stamps their own style on a particular sporting discipline.

Hovering with one leg

Hovering with one leg is the first step to advanced unicycling, and is based on propelling the unicycle with one pedal. Technically it resembles hovering with both legs (pages 84, 85). The difficulty, however, lies in applying the right amount of pressure with the active leg. It is also important to find a definite rhythm for the movement.

A unicycle with a 24" wheel or larger can at first be very energy sapping for your active leg. You can 'park' your free (inactive) leg in various positions, such as to the front, to the rear, to the side, behind you with your knee bent, on the frame or crossed over the active leg. You have achieved a certain mastery if you can change the position of the free leg without affecting the hovering action of the active one.

Hovering with one leg with various positions for the free leg

When learning to hover with one leg you must find a suitable support to hold onto. During the course of the practice session gradually try to reduce your dependence on this support. For those beginners who do not want to compromise there is also the possibility of removing one pedal from the crank. The drawback of this method, though, is that you do not learn to hold the free leg away from the danger area where the pedal would be revolving were it screwed in. Practise hovering with the left and the right leg alternately.

Go through the exercises described for hovering with both feet on the pedals, only this time with just one (page 86).

Practise hovering with one leg, holding the free leg in different positions. Try to change these positions as you hover.

Mounting

Depending on the nature of the technique that you are practising, you may have to dismount and re-mount many times. This is a good opportunity to try out different mounting techniques. For a while you should stop practising the techniques which you already do well and concentrate on others.

If mounting is built into another training programme, it is inadvisable to combine the practising of different mounting techniques with the main exercise. This extra practice is not a good idea if the mounting technique is new and you are still making a number of mistakes. Such techniques should be the focal point of a practice session. Your complete concentration should be directed towards learning this one new technique. Only when you have achieved a success rate of about a third to a half of all attempts with a particular mounting technique should you practise and perfect it in addition to learning other skills.

Mounting from the front

Begin by placing the unicycle behind you with the saddle between your legs. If you mount with the right foot on the pedal, hold the front of the saddle with your left hand. The right foot is placed on the right pedal, crank and pedal point towards you, angled to the floor (photo, left).

Mounting from the front: starting position

Your left foot should be flat on the ground. Bring your weight onto the right pedal by pushing up quickly and firmly with your left leg, forcing the right pedal into its lowest position (photo, right). Now move your left foot quickly upwards and catch the left pedal as it reaches its highest position (photo, right). You are ready to go.

With this exercise you will probably find that, to begin with, you are looking down between your wide-apart legs rather clumsily, neck bent, trying to find the right pedal position. However, after a bit of practice your foot "senses" the correct pedal position and you can do the mount with a straight neck.

> Mount from the front and begin hovering.

Mounting from the front

Mounting from the side

A stylish method of getting on the unicycle is the side-mount. Visually it resembles the normal mounting of a bicycle. If you want to mount from the left, set the left pedal in its lowest position and place your left foot on it. Hold the saddle with both hands, the left to the front. The frame should be almost vertical. Place your right foot at an angle to the wheel (photo below left). From this starting position push off firmly from the floor with your right leg and lift it over the saddle (your leg can be outstretched, but it is more difficult).

To make it easier getting on the saddle, incline the frame of the unicycle towards you a little (photo below right).

Side-mount:
After pushing off from the floor, lift your right leg over the saddle.

The trick is to prevent your arms resting on the saddle and pushing it to one side. This occurs in the unstable stage shortly after pushing upwards with the right leg.

Mount from the side and begin hovering.

After mounting from the side, ride forwards immediately without hovering once.

Variation of the side-mount: After pushing up from the floor, your right leg swings over in front of the saddle.

A small extension of the side-mount:
The leg is not bent but out-stretched as it swings over the saddle.

After mounting (swing your leg over in front of saddle) ride backwards immediately without hovering once.

With your leg almost out-stretched, swing it over in front of the saddle (photo, left). You can swing your leg at head-height, but do not forget to do some stretching exercises before-hand.

Another possibility with the side-mount. By holding the saddle at the front with one hand, you leave the other hand free to hold your juggling props.

Side mount on a turning unicycle. Here you push up from the floor with your right leg in such a way that you do a quarter turn (or more) standing only on the left pedal (photos left, top and bottom). In doing so you must keep your whole body as close as possible to the axis of rotation. Only at the end of the turn (photo below), not during it, do you climb on. This exercise is rather difficult - but still possible.

Mounting with one leg

The mounts from the front, from behind and from the side can also be done with one leg. One proviso is that you can hover confidently with one leg.

The one-legged mount from behind the unicycle is the easiest of the three. Place the saddle between your legs with the unicycle inclined towards you. Your right foot is on the right pedal, which should be angled towards you and the floor (photo left). Push up firmly with your left leg and begin hovering immediately with your right. This is important because it is only by hovering that you achieve the desired stability. At the same time you can place your left foot on the frame (photo left below) or in another position.

One-legged mount from behind the unicycle

For the one-legged mount from the front stand in front of the unicycle with the saddle between your legs. Place your right foot on the right pedal, which is angled towards you and the floor. Push up firmly with the left leg and immediately begin to hover with the right. The difficulty with this exercise initially is to get the unicycle in the correct starting position since you are unable to see it. If it is not positioned correctly it may veer off to one side and you will not be able to mount it. You might strain your neck a little at the beginning trying to check the position of the unicycle, but after a bit of practice you will get a feeling for the correct pedal position without having to twist your neck.

Starting position for the front mount with one leg. Begin hovering immediately after pushing up firmly with the left leg.

The one-legged mount from the side is performed just like the normal side-mount (see page 94), only place the right foot on the frame instead of the pedal. The left leg must begin hovering immediately after the right foot has left the ground.

Mount the unicycle with one leg, placing the free leg in different positions each time (see pages 90/91).

Jump mount

Technically speaking the jump mount presents no insurmountable problems for advanced unicyclists. The difficulty is plucking up the courage to make the jump. Before you do so, both you and the unicycle must be in the correct starting position. You should only practise this mount when you are able to bunny-hop a little on the unicycle. Only then will you get the feeling of applying equal weight to both pedals at the same time.

Stand behind the unicycle, one hand holding the saddle from the front. The cranks and pedals should be horizontal, with the right crank pointing towards you (photo below left). This is the position from which you will jump up with both legs. Firstly, your feet land on the pedals at the same time and absorb your body weight, followed immediately afterwards by your backside on the saddle (photo below right).

Jump mount

It may be helpful at the beginning to incline the frame towards you a little so that your jump is flatter and shorter. On the whole there are no exercises which will help you prepare for this trick. Even if you have prepared everything described above meticulously, you still have to make the decision when to jump. Full concentration, a good mastery of hovering with both legs and enthusiasm for practice will make it a little easier to perform this excellent trick successfully, and quite quickly it should become part of your standard repertoire.

> Do a jump mount, holding the saddle with your left and your right hand alternately.

> Do a jump mount and begin bunny-hopping immediately without hovering.

Jump mount
on a free-standing unicycle

When you have safely mastered the jump mount, you can practise it on a free-standing unicycle. The preparation for this trick is the same as for the jump-mount. With this mount you let go of the unicycle briefly, but only when it is standing exactly upright and remains still for a brief moment. At this point jump up immediately. In most cases a slight moment of hesitation will result in failure.

Kick-up mount

You have had to use your hands for all the mounting techniques described so far. With the kick-up mount the unicycle is lifted off the floor with the legs. To do this it must firstly be placed in a particular position on the floor with the right side facing upwards and the frame and crank forming an approximate right angle. Place your left foot under the saddle. With your right foot at the angle of the right pedal and the crank, push your body weight onto the right pedal along the line of the crank (this important stage is illustrated from two angles - see photos below and opposite). Through the pressure applied to the right pedal your body weight shifts from the left leg to the right. The unicycle moves towards the upright position, the left foot kicks the saddle into your inner right thigh (photo below right).

Starting position of the kick-up mount, seen from the side

Kick-up mount: the whole movement sequence seen from the front

Sit on the saddle and place the foot that made the kick–up on the left pedal (see photo 4, p.103). Try to raise and guide the saddle sensitively rather than give it a short, sharp kick.

This difficult technique requires a little patience - you are unlikely to learn it in a day. The following tips may make it easier:

- The kick-up mount often results in contact between the crank and your ankle bone. Wear ankle-high sports shoes if you practise this trick repeatedly.
- If, as often happens, the saddle is raised as desired but then falls quickly to the floor in front of your body again, you have probably brought your body weight too far forwards and not, as you should have done, to the side along the line of the crank.

Practise 100 kick-up mounts a day. Count the number of successful attempts and raise your success rate until it is constantly over 95%.

Dismount the unicycle backwards. As you do so bring it as gently as possible and without using your hands into the correct position for the next kick-up mount. Practise dismounting, kicking-up, dismounting etc. one after the other, without using your hands.

Bunny-hopping

Bunny-hopping on a unicycle is fun to do and very appealing to watch. On the other hand if you do not have a sturdy unicycle or you are a quite heavy, parts of the unicycle can break. Sometimes you also run the risk of injury.

Bunny-hopping on the spot

Slow down and bring the cranks into the horizontal position. If the saddle is at the correct height your legs should be slightly bent. By pushing firmly on the pedals with both feet at the same time, your body hops into the air. The difficulty is in applying even and simultaneous pressure on the pedals so that you jump directly upwards and land again in an upright position. You may have trouble with this to

begin with - your first few attempts will not be directly upwards, and by landing at an angle you will not be able to jump up again. You have to get through this stage, and an important breakthrough is achieved when you can do two jumps one after the other. Then you know that the first jump was correct.

Bunny-hopping on the unicycle

You must lift the unicycle into the air with you - if you jump up by yourself you will just land heavily on the saddle again. You can do this by holding on to the saddle with both hands, one at the front, the other at the back. A more stylish method is to hold on with just one hand (see photo p.105). You can keep both hands free if you manage to jump up holding the saddle firmly between your thighs. Here, a wider saddle is easier to grip. This is not, however, a fail-safe technique as sooner or later the unicycle will slip a little to the side.

The correct way of securing rider to unicycle. The strap goes under the saddle behind the seat-post and around the hips.

A good way to bunny-hop continuously is to tie a belt, cord or piece of rope around your hips and the saddle (photo, left). Whatever you use, make sure it is not elastic; the unicycle will spring up fractionally after you do and you will be hit by the saddle. Do not worry about tying yourself firmly to the unicycle. It is the best way to bunny-hop and causes you no problems, since the tension of the strap loosens if you fall and you do not remain lashed to the unicycle. Unless you can bunny-hop without thinking you should avoid securing your feet to the pedals.

Bunny-hop to musical rhythms of different tempos and synchronize your jumps to the beat.

Bunny-hop on the spot, holding the saddle with your right hand. Do the same exercise using the left hand, then with both hands.

Bunny-hop several times on the spot (left pedal to the front), then ride forwards a half-turn of the cranks, jump again several times (the right pedal is now to the front), ride forwards a half-turn of the crank and jump etc. The most difficult variation of this exercise is: one jump, forwards a half-turn, one jump, forwards a half-turn etc. Practise this riding both forwards and backwards.

Bunny-hop forwards, backwards and to the side.

Bunny-hopping with turns

When you have built up confidence, try bunny-hopping on the spot and turning at the same time. Begin with small turns, and progress to larger ones. To do this you will need to jump up off the ground quite vigorously because to change direction you need a bit of height. With practice you should manage to do 90° turns (quarter-turns). Everything over 90°, i.e. half-turns, three-quarter turns or even a full 360° turn is considerably more difficult.

Make a series of quarter-turns one after the other in the same direction.

Make a series of quarter-turns one after the other, changing direction.

With the smallest number of landings possible, do two complete revolutions on the unicycle by bunny-hopping.

With the smallest number of landings possible, do five complete revolutions on the unicycle by bunny-hopping.

Skipping

Rope skipping on a unicycle is not only difficult but also strenuous - it combines particularly well the aspects of co-ordination and conditioning. Not least for these reasons it is a big hit when performed in public. Two movements are combined for skipping on a unicycle, and it will be easier to learn if you can do these movements individually beforehand; bunny-hopping without the use of your hands and rope-skipping without the unicycle.

Hold the rope in both hands behind the body. Begin bunny-hopping on the spot just high enough to keep your balance. Swing the rope over your head to the front and jump up so that the rope can swing through under the wheel. Drop your hands down and a little to the side to prevent the rope from hitting the pedals.

The main difficulty is finding the right moment to make the first jump. It will take quite a few attempts to get this. Even if you do not succeed at first, remember that each attempt brings you nearer to your objective - not without good reason do they say you learn from your mistakes. Once you manage to clear the rope for the first time it will not be long before you find the definitive rhythm.

A strap gives good support for skipping on the unicycle.

If you can skip in the standard way - one jump with each pass of the rope - try other methods, for example by doing several jumps with each pass, by swinging the rope backwards, by crossing your arms, or, for top unicyclists, by doing one jump with two passes of the rope one after the other at lightning speed.

Skip 5, 10, 15, 20 or more times on the unicycle one after the other. Change the tempo. Skip very quickly, then very slowly, both with and without jumps in between passes of the rope.

Turn around slowly on the spot as you skip.

Vary the skipping by crossing your arms, swinging the rope backwards etc.

Jumping up and down steps

Step jumping is an impressive trick, but also a dangerous one. It allows you to negotiate obstacles which otherwise would bar your progress. You should only practise this trick if you are able to bunny-hop and turn at the same time. Before you tackle proper flights of steps, practise jumping up and down a single one, preferably a small kerb near a driveway. Ride up to the kerb, making sure the wheel and the kerb are parallel to each other, and begin bunny-hopping on the spot before making the decisive jump upwards. If after a little practice this jump presents no problems, try jumping up and down the kerb continually and rhythmically. If you can also jump high kerbs safely, it is time to test your newly acquired ability on a proper flight of steps.

Wide (stone) steps which are not too high are good for practising on. Initially the steps should offer enough space for you to hover on or to dismount if need be. Set yourself realistic goals which you can achieve without falling off. It is better not to take unnecessary risks. Only move onto the next exercise when you feel confident enough. Begin each exercise on the lowest step of a flight.

Prepare for jumping up flights of steps by practising up and down a kerb.

Jump up 3, 5, 10 or more steps. Do several jumps on each step. End each exercise with as controlled a dismount as possible.
Jump up 3, 5, 10 or more steps. Jump just once on each step. End the exercise with a controlled dismount.

Jump down 1, 3, 5, 10 or more steps. Only increase the number of steps when you feel really confident. Jump several times on each step. End the exercise with a controlled dismount.

Jump down 1, 3, 5, 10 or more steps. Only increase the number of steps when you feel confident. Jump just once on each step. End the exercise with a controlled dismount.

You should only combine jumping up and jumping down a large number of steps when you are totally confident you can do each discipline individually.
You cannot ride up steps - you have to jump up them. It is possible to ride down them, but this is a very dangerous exercise.

A difficult achievement to beat in this area was established by a French unicyclist in 1971, who went up the 1700 steps or so of the Eiffel Tower in Paris. In doing so, it is said, he did not fall off or hold on to the railings once (Wiley, 1984, p.186).

Skipping and step jumping on a unicycle, illustrated here by Gerd Waree, are extremely difficult to combine. Take care if trying to copy it! Though here it appears easy, it is very dangerous and requires years of practice under professional conditions.

Other tricks

Riding with one leg

Riding with just the one (pedalling) leg is a difficult and extraordinary trick. To learn it well you have to practise every day for several weeks.

You will learn this trick more quickly if, as you did when learning to ride the unicycle, you practise with two people to assist you for the first few attempts. Even if you have become a good unicyclist in the meantime, do not be embarrassed to practise with people assisting you again - it is worth it.

A helpful exercise for learning to ride with one leg.

If you have help at the beginning with the problems of balance and impetus, you can concentrate on a rhythmical leg movement. Apply firm pressure on the pedal, though not too much, and control the unicycle without braking heavily on the pedal as it rises. You are more stable if you place your free (inactive) leg on the frame as you ride along. After this initial session with help, practising by yourself later will be less frustrating, for by then you should be able to complete at least a few revolutions .

Riding with one leg

When you begin practising this trick by yourself it is advisable, before taking one foot from the pedal, to set off normally with a smooth and even pedal action. Then push one pedal down slightly harder on the last revolution of the crank before removing your other foot from the pedal. If you compare the position of the crank with the hand on a clock, then the inactive foot is removed from the pedal at the moment when the crank on the pedalling leg is showing just after one o'clock. Do not to go too slowly.

When the pedalling leg reaches this position, the other foot is removed from the pedal. The arrow shows the direction of travel.

At first you will manage only a few revolutions, and the unicycle will probably veer slightly in the direction of the pedalling leg. When learning you will probably encounter the following problems:

− Your balance will go to pieces.
− You keep your balance but you come to a halt without sufficient impetus.

It may help to ride down a gentle incline to reduce the impetus problem slightly.

With increased practice you will be able to cover longer and longer distances. When you can do this confidently, you can try other exercises:

Ride around a slalom course of small obstacles.
Ride as slowly as possible.
Ride in large circles to the right and left, then later smaller ones.
Hover on one leg and begin riding forwards, still with just the one leg.
Perform a figure-of-eight. The aim is to gradually reduce the size of the 'eight' as much as you possibly can.

As with hovering on one leg, you can place the free leg in various positions when doing this trick, though it is considerably more difficult than when hovering. You can view the next practice exercise either as a challenge or a suggestion, as the case may be.

Ride along with one leg, changing the position of the free leg as you do so (see pages 90/91).

Riding without sitting on the saddle

With this technique you bring most of your body weight onto the pedals rather than the saddle. You will feel the change as you ride along, especially in the leg muscles.

The exercises in this 'standing position' work the leg muscles considerably harder than the exercises 'sitting down'. If for any reason you have problems sitting down, then you can try riding the unicycle using this method.

You will often have to dismount when learning this trick. In doing so you can avoid injury by straddling the unicycle.

Saddle in front of the body

The biggest problem to begin with is getting into the starting position and holding onto the saddle, which sways considerably as you pedal. The starting position is as follows: you have both feet on the pedals and you hold the saddle with one hand. There are a number of ways of getting into this position.

1. Hold the unicycle by the saddle in front of your body with your more dexterous hand. With your other hand hold on to a suitable support and climb onto the unicycle.

2. Ride along, and choosing a moment when the cranks are in the horizontal position, stand up briefly and pull the saddle forwards.

3. Free-mount: Place the unicycle in front of you with the right pedal in its lowest position. Grip the right side of the saddle with your right hand. Put your right foot on the right pedal (photo p.116, top) and push up from the floor with your left leg (photo p.116 below). At this point the unicycle moves sharply in the direction of the pedal with the load on it, the right in this case. So that the unicycle remains exactly upright, you must apply counter pressure to the saddle with your right hand. Place your left foot on the left pedal and set off.

Once in the starting position you will learn firstly to ride forwards. For this you can proceed with the familiar 'one helper' method. The helper holds your free hand and supports you. If you are learning solo you can try to feel your way along a fixed support (wall, fence etc). If you want to try it without support, or there is none available, you will only manage a few revolutions to begin with. You will master this technique sooner and better if you do not practice too doggedly.

Free-mount, holding saddle in front of body

Ride forwards, holding the saddle with your right hand, then your left hand, then with both hands. If you feel confident change hands as you go along.

Practise mounting and hovering in all possible variations without sitting on the saddle, alternating between the right and left pedal in the lowest position and your right and left hand on the saddle.

Do zigzags, slaloms and turns.

Ride backwards with the saddle in front of the body (photo, below), do zigzags, slaloms and turns.

Bring the cranks into the horizontal position and bunny-hop without sitting on the saddle.

Riding backwards, holding the saddle in front of your body.

Riding with your chest on the saddle.

Saddle behind the body

With this technique you hold the saddle behind your body with one hand, and your body weight rests on the pedals. It is not too difficult, provided you can ride with the saddle in front of your body. The learning procedure and the practice exercises correspond to those with the saddle in front of the body (see page 115 ff).

Riding with the saddle behind your body

Upper body (chest) on the saddle

With this technique you do not hold the saddle in your hands. Bring most of your body weight via your chest onto the saddle to prevent the unicycle from swaying and to keep it steady.

> Ride along with your chest on the saddle and change the position of your arms as you do so (around the saddle, hands behind neck, hands on knees etc).

> Hover with your chest on the saddle.

Pirouettes

If you can turn sharply and ride in tight circles, it is time to have a go at the pirouette. With the pirouette the unicycle rotates around the vertical axis of the body. There are several ways of performing pirouettes, but basically you can do them either by pedalling or without pedalling.

One way to do a pirouette as you pedal is to ride in ever decreasing circles until you are virtually riding on the spot, revolving around the axis of rotation. This is quite strenuous and you can go dizzy after several turns, so take a rest before trying it again.

Ride in circles with as small a diameter as possible (smaller than one metre).

Another way is to perform a pirouette without pedal action. If you want to perform it to the left, slow down until the pedals are horizontal with the right pedal to the front. If the left pedal were to the front, there would be a great temptation to push down on it in support of the pirouette.
Now stretch round as far as possible in the opposite direction with both arms, that is to the right (photo p.120, left). You then swing your upper body immediately to the left. This swing should be transferred to the lower half of the body so that you turn with the unicycle on the spot (photo p.120, right). The pedals move as little as possible during this exercise, if at all. The tyre marks give you some indication about the quality of the pirouette. Ideally you should turn on a very small spot about the size of a coin. The trick is easier with a well-inflated tyre and a flat surface since the friction between the tyre and the floor is reduced.

The pirouette without pedalling:
Reach back in one direction, then swing in the other.

Do a 90° pirouette, or further, without pedalling.

Do several pirouettes one after the other without pedalling. Swing your arms back, pirouette, swing your arms back, pirouette etc. as often as you can without dismounting.

It is also possible to perform a mixed pirouette. Begin the first series of spins by riding in tight circles, then hold the subsequent pirouette without pedalling.

Wheel-walking

Walking the wheel is riding the unicycle without using the pedals. If you can master this trick well, you can justifiably count yourself a member of a very select group of unicycle experts.

When you wheel-walk you propel the unicycle by contact of the shoe against the tyre. Consequently your leg movements resemble those of walking backwards: Place one foot on the tyre as near as possible to the frame and extend the leg forwards. As you do so, draw the other foot back to the frame, keeping your body weight on the saddle. Shoe soles and tyre should both grip well and not be worn down.

The best way to begin wheel-walking is to find a narrow space in which you can support yourself from both sides, i.e. between two fences. It is not quite so easy to learn it with support from just one side. If you decide to learn with two helpers, they should make sure they have a lot of time to spare. To learn wheel-walking you will need a good few attempts - it is not something you learn in a day, in fact you will probably have to practise for weeks, if not months. Think of the frustrating lack of success you had at the beginning: practice makes perfect, and each little bit brings you a step nearer your goal.

Learning to wheel-walk during the initial stages: Support from both sides

Wheel-walking

After a little practice you will be able to go the first few metres without support. At this stage the following tips may help you:

• Wheel walking is a guiding of the wheel for as long as possible with each foot alternately. The active foot is placed with the front of the shoe on the tyre and is rolled along up to the heel. A short, heavy push of the foot on the wheel does not give you control.

• Do not go too fast. If you go too fast, you go faster than the wheel, you start to lean forwards, and you have to go faster and faster for the unicycle to keep up with you. After a few metres you cannot go any faster and you fall off. If this happens you fall forwards (no problem) and you can usually reach back and grab hold of the saddle.

• Go slow, but not too slow. Slower walking is more controlled walking, though if you are too slow, the unicycle becomes unstable and gently topples over to the side. When you walk slowly, you are slower than the unicycle and therefore a little behind it and the walking then resembles more of a braking movement of the speeding unicycle. If you fall off in this position the unicycle can catapult a long way forwards and you fly backwards, usually landing on both feet but, in the worst cases, on your backside.

The skill of wheel walking is finding the right speed. Try not to get too far forward or too far back. The tendency for controlled wheel-walking is to lean back ever so slightly. If you can vary your speed you will have achieved good control of wheel-walking.

Hold onto a suitable support, take your feet off the pedals and place them on the tyre. Begin walking the wheel from this position.
Begin wheel walking from a hovering position and from hovering on one leg.
Walk the wheel slowly and quickly alternately.
Walk the wheel, making right turns, left turns, slalom etc.

Letting the unicycle glide

When wheel-walking you do not let the tyre roll; the feet guide the unicycle rather than restrict it. If you can walk over 20 consecutive metres on it, you will notice that the tyre occasionally slips a few centimetres under the sole of your shoe, thus acting as a brake. This is another way of controlling the unicycle.

Since wheel-walking involves alternately guiding and braking on the tyre, it is possible to brake at any time if and when it is necessary. Braking is achieved in this way by the tyre constantly dragging on the sole of the shoe. This sliding of the tyre on the sole is one of the most difficult things to do on a unicycle. If you stop applying this sensitive braking movement, the unicycle can fly rather a long way forwards. If you let the unicycle glide for about half a metre you are already quite accomplished - everything over and above this marks you as an absolute top unicyclist. You are almost perfect, but not quite.

Wheel-walk faster and faster and brake sensitively by letting the soles slip on the tyre.
Go from wheel-walking to letting the unicycle glide. Measure it so that you can cover longer stretches with this gliding technique.

Special tricks on the unicycle

If you master the techniques described in this book soundly on both sides of your body, you are an excellent unicyclist. Of course many other unicycle tricks are possible. Many of them are very difficult and cannot usually be learnt by amateurs in a reasonable period of time. They remain predominantly the domain of a handful of artists and professional unicyclists. However, for those who wish to try, here are some suggestions:

- ❏ Ride backwards with one leg and change the position of the free one.
- ❏ Do a jump mount backwards onto the unicycle.
- ❏ Wheel-walk backwards.
- ❏ Wheel-walk sideways with both hands on the saddle and the feet left and right of the frame.
- ❏ Wheel-walk with the saddle in front of or behind your body.
- ❏ Wheel-walk with just one leg or even with your hands.
- ❏ Gain some momentum by riding forwards with one leg, take the pedalling foot from the pedal as well and place it on the frame so that the unicycle runs freely.
- ❏ Hold the saddle in both hands (or just one) and ride with just one foot on the pedal.
- ❏ Set off, holding the saddle behind you. Let go of it so that it falls to the floor and continue pedalling.
- ❏ Ride along holding the saddle in front of you, pause with the cranks horizontal and jump up from both pedals at the same time, quickly twist the unicycle round while you are in the air and land safely again on the pedals.
- ❏ Ride backwards down steps.
- ❏ The rather difficult pirouette is made more difficult by riding backwards and performing it.

Sharing the fun - Unicycling with other people

Unicycling is not exclusively a sport for individuals; some forms of co-participation are also possible - and are fun. Most communal activities contain the notion of working together and less the notion of sporting conflict, though in some games where you compete against one another the weaker participants are also given a chance and the rules are arranged accordingly. Unicyclists should not be divided into winners and losers - if you can all win, then everyone will have fun.

Unicycling together

Basically, there are two different ways of unicycling with other people; riding with and without body contact.

Unicycling with body contact means you can support your partner by linking arms or holding hands. Learning different techniques (forwards, backwards, riding in circles) is easier if you can support each other. More acrobatic riding, with someone on your shoulders, requires an extremely sound riding technique, a sturdy unicycle and a light partner.

Riding in circles: sometimes better in two's

The exercise 'wheelbarrows' can be a lot of fun. Here you lie with your stomach on the saddle and move forwards by turning the pedals with your hands. Your position is improved considerably if you turn the saddle round 90 degrees. To begin with you need four people to stabilize the wheelbarrow - two on the side, level with the saddle, and one on each leg. It can also be more comfortable to pad out the saddle. If things do not work out at the beginning try lowering the saddle or tensing the muscles so that your body is as rigid as possible.

You will have to practise for a while before you can 'wheelbarrow' with just two people pushing your legs (or even just one person, also riding a unicycle). 'Free wheelbarrowing', ie without any help, is the pinnacle of athletic achievement and is very rarely attained. Anyone who can do this is in a position to think about performing for money.

When unicycling without body contact you can try the following exercises:

Racing: Cover a predetermined stretch as fast as possible. The unicycle record for 100m is 14.89 seconds (Kümmel, H.-H 1990, p.218).

Shadow riding: One rider sets off and another rider, following at set distance, must imitate everything the leader does as precisely as possible. After a certain period of time, or when the rider in front touches the ground, the other unicyclist takes over the role of leader.

Mirror image: Two unicyclists hover opposite each other. The actions of one rider must be imitated by the other as a mirror image. Again, change roles after a certain period of time or by touching the floor.

Parallel slalom: As in skiing, two identical slalom courses can be laid out next to each other. Use small stones or something similar to mark out the course. The winner is the quickest rider, though the loser reserves the right to lay out the next slalom course.

Swapping unicycles: An exchange of unicycles, especially if the wheel sizes are different, is usually an enlightening experience. Changing the height of the saddle can also provide a new experience in riding a unicycle.

Games

When several unicyclists meet up together, it would seem absurd to suppress the natural instinct for playing merely because you are all sitting on unicycles. You can play different games depending on the number and creativity of the participants. Here are some suggestions:

Tag: The boundaries of the playing area must be clearly defined. One rider starts off and tries to tag another rider. Whoever is tagged must try as quickly as possible to tag someone else.

Don't touch me!: Two riders compete, trying to touch each other while trying to avoid being touched themselves. All contacts (other than below the elbow) count as points. The game is best in a smaller playing area.

Chains: At least three unicyclists form a chain by linking arms (photo right). With an uneven number of people the person in the middle can practise a pirouette, provided that the ends of the chain move in opposite directions. If the chain is long enough one end can try and catch up with the other.

Other suitable possibilities are games involving the throwing and passing of something, like a ball or a Frisbee, for example, or even unicycle badminton.

The ends of the chain move in opposite directions, rotating the rider in the middle on the spot.

Another possibility is to play team games with a ball (e.g. hockey, basketball). You are free to play them how you wish, but it is better if you agree upon some rules beforehand, such as the playing time, the method of scoring, the penalties for dismounting and the nature and method of manipulating the ball. The playing time and method of scoring can be agreed quite quickly. The penalty for dismounting could be, for example, possession to the other team and a free throw from the point at which the opposing player touched the floor with a foot. You could move the ball by dribbling with it, making sure that it touches the ground at least once every second or third revolution of the crank. If you cannot dribble the ball, or you are not allowed to, you could have a rule whereby the ball must be passed at the latest after 1, 2, 3, 4 or more revolutions of the crank. All such games depend on a gathering of many unicyclists and consequently require a certain degree of organisation.

Outings

A particular kind of sociable and environmentally-friendly recreational activity is a unicycle trip. Long trips require a certain amount of planning. The following information with regard to the speed of unicycles in continuous operation may help you plan a trip: A 20" wheel is equivalent to a pedestrian walking briskly, about 4 mph; a 24" wheel approximately to someone jogging, about 7 mph.

This information does not relate to maximum speeds, it serves only as a rough guide and can vary considerably from person to person. Some unicycle records give an indication of the kind of performances which are possible in extreme cases: The relationship between running and unicycling is illustrated with a comparison of their individual 24 hour endurance records: 24-hour running record: 276.2 km, 24-hour unicycling record: 232.5 km (from the Guinness Book of Records 1991, Kümmel, H.-H.1990, 9, p.218).

With regard to longer trips, the journey of U.Thiedemann in 1984 is one of several record attempts on a unicycle. The distance covered from the Atlantic coast of France to Hanover in Germany was almost 1600 km and was completed in only 13 days (August, H. 1989, p.29). A daily average of over 120 km proves that in extreme cases unicycle and rider can also go the distance.

With his trip in the Alps in 1989 G.Frey from Switzerland showed not only endurance and skill, but also confirmed the climbing ability of the unicycle. In 13 hours 45 minutes he covered a distance of 105 km, overcoming in the process an altitude difference of about 4100 metres. Under these extreme conditions he achieved an average speed of 11 km/hr (Kümmel, H.-H. 1990, p.218).

Most trips, however, turn out to be rather more modest. To make yours successful, here are a few tips:

- Embarking on a trip by yourself can be fine, but it is more fun with a group of people.
- Before you set off, establish a route of feasible length, preferably over cycle paths etc. and away from traffic.
- Your speed is first and foremost determined by the size of the wheel, how fast you pedal, and your riding ability. Other factors, however, such as obstacles, hills, other pedestrians and cyclists, the surface of the track itself and the weather can also have a decisive influence on how fast you are able to go.
- Any important items (replacement parts, provisions etc) can be easily carried if there are several pairs of shoulders available. Rucksacks are excellent for this as it is best to keep your hands free when unicycling.

Giraffe Unicycles

Riding a Giraffe unicycle has advantages and disadvantages. The advantages are that it is fun to ride high above other cyclists and that the public are continually impressed by it. The disadvantages are that it is generally a difficult form of cycling and the possibilities to use it beyond the stage and the practice space are limited. The Giraffe is especially suitable for anyone who wants to perform shows.

Before you try to ride a Giraffe, there are a few things you should be aware of:

- It is easier than you might think, so have no false inhibitions.
- Due to the height of the saddle and the greater falling distance you have a different feeling from riding a standard unicycle. Falling off forwards or backwards is generally not a problem. Falls to the side can be dangerous.
- You need a lot of space. At the beginning choose your practice space so that you can fall to all sides without risk. Do not cycle around people or objects if you do not feel confident.
- It is no more difficult keeping your balance on a Giraffe than it is on a small unicycle - in fact it is even easier.
- You no longer propel the unicycle directly through the spindle of the wheel but via one or two chains. If the number of teeth differs on the two chain cogs you will experience a change in the gear ratio.

**From the left: Mini-giraffe with rather jerky riding qualities, 6'
Giraffe, 5' Giraffe.**

This means that one revolution of the crank does not correspond to
one revolution of the wheel and consequently you will have to get
used to the handling. Therefore, the way you ride a Giraffe unicycle is
affected by the number of teeth on the chain cogs.

133

- Before you attempt to ride a Giraffe, you should master all the basic techniques of unicycling. One proviso for free-mounting a Giraffe, for example, is to be able to do a side mount on a standard unicycle (see page 94).
- Not only is the sitting position more 'majestic', but so is the riding performance. Because of its length a Giraffe unicycle tolerates greater deviation from its supporting base, thereby giving you more time to make corrections.

The power transmission on a Giraffe is normally via one or two chains. Propulsion via several wheels is also possible but is rare (photo opposite, far right). Whether one or two chains is the best alternative is predominantly a matter of taste. Some unicyclists swear by two chains, others are absolutely convinced that one is sufficient. There are unicycles on offer with different wheel sizes and saddle heights. When starting off a 20" wheel is recommended.

The riding characteristics are influenced not only by the wheel size, but also by the number of teeth on the chain cogs. With the same number of teeth on the two cogs you cycle a 1:1 ratio (as with a standard unicycle). If the lower cog is bigger than the higher one, and has more teeth, the wheel turns less than once with every revolution of the crank. The pedalling is very light but covers little distance. Cogs the other way round (top one bigger, bottom one smaller) lead to opposite riding characteristics. One revolution of the cranks results in more than one revolution of the wheel, and as a result the pedalling is heavier but covers more distance. With the right combination of cogs, for example, a sluggish 24" wheel can resemble a 20" wheel in riding performance.

Among the Giraffes on offer are those with the saddle at 150 cm (5', small Giraffes) and 180 cm (6' normal Giraffes), though you can also get them with saddle heights of 100 cm, 140 cm and 160 cm. All Giraffes with the saddle higher than 180 cm are for real specialists.

From the left: A neat solution - detachable seat-post for transportation. The other pieces of equipment are only for specialists: tall Giraffe; unicycle without saddle and frame, also known as an 'Ultimate wheel'; Giraffe propelled by a stack of three wheels rather than a chain.

It can be quite a struggle free-mounting a Giraffe unicycle. So that the start of your career on the Giraffe is not adversely affected by 'mounting frustration', get some riding experience first and postpone the difficult problem of the free-mount. After you have mounted the unicycle with help (page 137), try to cover a few metres with one or two people walking along beside you (if they are tall enough). After a short time you will be able to manage without help. It is not a case of having to learn afresh, but rather to re-learn a little.

Build up confidence by riding about on the Giraffe.

You will only manage to free-mount the Giraffe when you can confidently ride around on it first. Depending on how well you ride a small unicycle, practise around 5 to 20 hours of just riding forwards, backwards, hovering and turning etc (photo above). In these early stages ask someone to help you mount the unicycle.

Mounting the Giraffe

Mounting with help

For this you need some kind of support which is the right height for you to climb up and from where you can mount the unicycle without difficulty. This can be a fixed-frame ladder, a wall or gym wall-bars. Move onto the saddle from your support, bring one pedal into its lowest position and begin hovering. As you do so keep hold of the support to start with. Let go of the support and set off only when you feel absolutely ready.

Alternatively, your helpers can perform a strong-man act and raise you onto the unicycle. To do this place the wheel in front of an object to act as a brake, sit in a bent position on the saddle and tense your muscles so that your body is rigid. The helpers (at least two) lift and push you upwards. They should hold onto the unicycle until you are confident enough to hover or ride off by yourself.

It is also possible for you to climb up onto the unicycle supported by two helpers. The helpers stand to the left and right of the unicycle, holding it by the seat-post and using their feet as braking blocks to stop the wheel rolling forwards or backwards. From behind the unicycle, step firstly on to the tyre with one foot, then on to the pedal in its lowest position with the other foot, and sit on the saddle.

Only when you have gained some riding experience, and are familiar with the way a Giraffe handles, are you advised to practise the free-mount. There are several ways to do it:

Mounting via the pedal

This is the easiest way of mounting a Giraffe. However, it is really only possible if your unicycle is not higher than 6' (about 180 cm) and you yourself are taller than 1.80 metres. If you are shorter than this, or the unicycle taller, then this mount will be difficult, assuming your arms and legs are of average proportion. Whether or not you are tall enough to do this mount will become obvious when you take up the starting position.

**Mounting via the pedal:
Starting position**

Stand behind the unicycle with your right foot on the floor. Place your left foot on the pedal. The knee of your left leg should be held as high as possible. Hold the saddle at the front and back with both hands. From this position push up from the floor with your right leg. The left leg now takes on the important remainder of the work. Straighten it quickly and move swiftly onto the saddle. When straightening the left leg the power is directed straight upwards. Every force directed away from the unicycle is a mistake which will lead to failure. The mount is largely brought about by your legs; your hands support the movement by exerting downward pressure on the saddle.

Pressure should be exerted directly downwards (by the hands) and upwards (by the legs). Any attempt to pull yourself onto the saddle with your arms, thereby causing sideways pressure on the saddle, will fail because the whole unicycle is forced to the side. If you have avoided all the errors and manage to sit on the saddle, immediately place your right foot on the right pedal and begin hovering.

After your right foot has left the ground and before you place it on the right pedal, you can only control the unicycle with your left foot on the left pedal. Your chances of controlling the unicycle during this unstable stage are greater if you can hover with one leg.

Mounting via the pedal

Due to the strenuous starting position of this mount, prepare your leg and gluteal muscles with some stretching exercises so that you achieve the necessary flexibility and avoid injury.

Mounting via the tyre

With this method you use the tyre as a step ladder. Stand behind the unicycle with your left foot on the floor. Place your right foot on the tyre, with the point of your foot touching the frame to prevent the wheel from rolling.

Mounting via the tyre

Before you climb up make sure the left crank is in its lowest position. The actual mount begins by pushing off the floor with your left leg. Place it quickly on the left pedal (photo right) and straighten it immediately. This should bring you onto the saddle. Finally place your right foot on the right pedal (photo next page).

Initially the technique as described above is unlikely to go completely smoothly. Some tips may assist you here:

• Try not to pull yourself up with your arms. They should only hold the saddle, not push or pull it to the side.
• Try to do the mount quickly and without hesitation. The objective is to get on the saddle - you do not have time to pause midway and reflect.
• Go directly upwards when you push up from the tyre and the pedal.
• Before each attempt give yourself a command sequence, for example: push up, place foot, sit down. Recognize errors and change the commands according-ly, for example: keep arms loose, do not push saddle away.

The first successful mount you complete is a big breakthrough of which you can be proud. But from this memorable moment onwards there is still considerable work to do before you have the mount tight. Your success rate to begin with will be about 1 in 25, in other words, you need on average 25 attempts to complete one successful mount. When, after a great deal of practice, your success rate reaches about 1 in 5, you are becoming quite good, and when it reaches 1 in 2 and bet-ter you are very good.

Riding and learning tricks

Most of the tricks which can executed on a small unicycle can also be performed on a Giraffe. The differences in technique vary only slightly, not fundamentally. Riding forwards and backwards, hovering, bunny-hopping, riding with one leg etc. are all equally possible on a Giraffe. Some tricks, though, are ruled out because of the distance between saddle and tyre, like wheel-walking, for example. The techniques for mounting the Giraffe are basically different and also more difficult.

Learning the techniques on a Giraffe follows the same principle as on a small unicycle. The main advantage on a small one is that you gain experience of riding without the fear of injury. Transferring the skills you have learned on a small unicycle to a Giraffe is simply a matter of repeating the same exercises which you performed in order to learn particular techniques on the small unicycle. The sequence of practice exercises remains mostly unchanged.

Faking

A special feature of riding a Giraffe is faking. Faking gives the impression that you are about to fall off at every moment. Of course you do not fall off - as if by chance, you always regain control at the last moment. By bending forwards as far as possible, which looks particularly dangerous on a Giraffe, you can impressively simulate a near-fall. The greater the angle of the unicycle, the more enthralled the spectators will be. The desired impression of an impending or narrowly avoided fall can be enhanced by waving your arms about wildly, by a terrified facial expression or by desperate cries for help.

Playing the role of the hapless beginner who only just manages to avoid accidents and catastrophies requires a very sound mastery of the Giraffe. Before faking in front of the public all the movements should be practised thoroughly. The joke is lost if you do actually fall off.

Dismounting

A controlled session on the Giraffe ends with a voluntary dismount. For this you can jump off in front of or behind the unicycle. Since the unicycle moves forwards or backwards when dismounting, you need a bit of space to perform it.

When dismounting to the front, lean forwards a little, hold onto the saddle and jump down with your knees bent. You should land almost exactly on the spot where the unicycle was before you began your dismount. As you drop down almost vertically, the unicycle rolls back behind you.

When dismounting behind the unicycle lean back slightly and drop down. Hold onto the unicycle and it will roll forwards.

When dismounting to the front hold the saddle and bend the knees to cushion the fall.

Juggling on the Unicycle

When unicycling your hands are free. You can clap, wave, shuffle cards or whistle with your fingers. However, unicycling also lends itself to all activities broadly connected with juggling: juggling with different objects (scarves, balls, rings, clubs, fruit, eggs, small stones etc), ball and plate spinning, juggling with cigar boxes, diabolo and devil stick. It is equally possible to combine unicycling with yo-yoing, rope swinging or bubble blowing.

Unicycling and juggling is very watchable. In the next section the basic techniques of juggling are explained to teach you to juggle successfully on a unicycle. If you can already juggle three balls in the basic cascade you can skip this section.

Learning to juggle

Before you attempt to juggle on a unicycle, it is better to learn to juggle under more favourable conditions - i.e. standing on terra firma. Objects can be thrown and caught in all sorts of ways. There are many patterns which differ both in appearance and in difficulty. The first step to juggling on a unicycle is to learn the basic juggling pattern, the cascade. To learn it, get ready to do the following exercises:

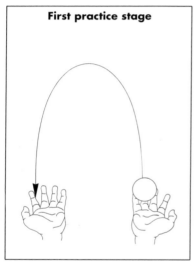
First practice stage

Preparation

You need three objects of the same size and weight (tennis ball size), which preferably will not roll too far when dropped. To juggle you should hold your arms as if you are holding a tray at waist height. So that you do not throw the balls too far forwards, practise in front of a wall.

One-ball practice: Throw a juggling ball from the right hand to the left and back again. The throw should be approximately forehead height.

Two-ball practice (see diagram above right): Hold a ball in each hand. Throw ball 1 from the right hand. When this ball has reached its highest point (about forehead height), throw ball 2 from the left hand to the right hand. Begin each attempt from the right hand and the left hand alternately.

Second practice stage

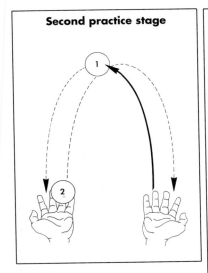

Third practice stage

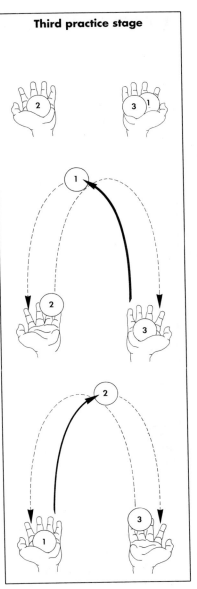

Three-ball practice: Start with two balls in the right hand and one ball in the left (diagram top right). Throw ball 1 from the right hand. When this ball has reached its highest point, throw ball 2 from the left hand (diagram centre right). Catch ball 1 with the left hand, which is now free. When ball 2 has reached its highest point, throw ball 3 (diagram bottom right). Catch ball 2 with the right hand, which is now free, and throw ball 1 again from the left hand etc. If you succeed in doing this continuously you can juggle three balls in the basic cascade.

You should keep practising the cascade until you can do it well and without a great deal of concentration. You have reached the desired level when you can look through the juggling pattern and watch television, for example.

Only when you have learnt to juggle the basic cascade (standing on the ground) should you combine juggling with unicycle tricks. If you go through the practice exercises marked with (J) when going forwards, backwards and hovering, you will learn to juggle systematically on the unicycle.

The exercises relate to combining different riding techniques on the unicycle and the cascade. Other patterns, of which there are many, are not discussed within the framework of this book. However, if you want to improve further, you can do this by:

- Inventing new jugging patterns.
- Learning more juggling patterns from books, or having them explained and demonstrated to you by jugglers. There is a wide range of specialist books on juggling available from bookshops and juggling shops and there are juggling clubs in most towns.
- Combining any other patterns you know with your unicycle tricks, or, if possible, juggling with more than three objects.

Combining juggling and unicycling

You should be able to do both activities automatically, that is, each movement (e.g. hovering on the unicycle and juggling with 3 balls) should be executed without too much thought or effort. This is important because initially the "movement computer" in the brain is completely concentrated on avoiding the mutual disturbance of both movements by each other. So if you notice that combining them is not working because you are making simple errors with either the juggling or the unicycling, it would make sense to improve each activity individually.

Juggling on the unicycle begins in combination with the most simple riding technique, going forwards. Gradually move on to more difficult techniques, like riding slalom courses and riding in circles etc. However, the essence of juggling on a unicycle is to combine it with hovering. The degree of difficulty can be varied by hovering, by hovering on one leg with the free leg in various positions, by performing different juggling patterns or by varying the nature (rings, clubs) and number of the juggling props.

Practice and training tips

- Before you juggle on the unicycle, warm up by juggling and unicycling individually.
- On a unicycle you juggle in a sitting position. It may be helpful, therefore, to practise juggling sitting down before you try it on a unicycle.
- Each new juggling pattern on the unicycle is initially an unfamiliar action which causes a considerable disturbance to your sense of balance and to which you must become accustomed. So do not despair if you frequently have to dismount when you practise a new juggling pattern.

Mounting

You can basically perform all the mounts if your hands are free of juggling props. You can put small juggling balls in your pockets or have them thrown to you by another person. When mounting the unicycle with clubs or rings, holding them in one hand leaves the other hand free. In this case the following mounting techniques are most suited:

- Side mount with one hand (p.96)
- Kick-up mount (p. 102/103)
- Jump mount (p.100)

Picking up juggling props

When juggling on the unicycle your props will sooner or later fall to the floor. To pick them up, however, you should not dismount and reveal to everyone that something has gone wrong. If you do manage to pick up the props you can turn a small slip up into a success. For people with normal body proportions who do not have arms like Orang-Utans, picking up from the floor on the unicycle is not that easy at first and not always without pain.

Ride slowly up to your juggling prop and bend forwards as far as possible. Since your body is inclined so far forwards in this position, you must make sure that the frame of the unicycle is angled backwards a little in order to keep your balance. Bending down may be easier if you simultaneously breath out.

Picking up juggling props

Unicycling is also a circus skill usually performed in conjunction with juggling or balancing other objects. You may have already observed some of these top tricks on the unicycle with great admiration. Unicycle displays by circus artists are the result of years and years of practice under professional conditions. Even a very good amateur cannot compete with this. The following examples illustrate what is possible:

Roman Bait - one-wheel juggler (1953)

Ernest Montego (1960)

**This, however, is quite possible for amateurs:
Club-passing on Giraffe unicycles.**

Unicycling and Physics

Some of the basic problems of unicycling can be explained with the aid of physics. Since there are no formulas or calculations in the following text, you do not need to have studied physics to read on:

Problems of balance

An upright unicycle without a rider falls over. In physics the brief moment of equilibrium of the free standing unicycle is very graphically called labile (from the Latin: labilis - to slip, slide). All bodies, including unicycles, endeavour to take up a stable balanced state (Latin: stabilis - steady), in this case falling over and lying down. Expressed in terms of physics, a falling body loses potential energy and gains kinetic energy, its centre of gravity sinks, and in our example the unicycle tips over. When lying down it has a stable balanced state and from such a position of low potential energy cannot move back by itself to the unstable position of equilibrium.

To return it to the unstable position it must be picked up - which means work must be done. Work must also be done when you ride a unicycle and keep it in a state of equilibrium; it is in balance.

This balancing act is dependent on the centre of gravity of the rider-unicycle unit lying vertically over the point of support. The centre of gravity of a simple body (e.g. a sphere) is exactly in the middle. With a person standing upright the centre of gravity lies somewhere between the navel and the spinal column.

One way or another, balancing depends on bringing the point of support (arrow) vertically under the centre of gravity (dot).
The figure on the left is balancing 'from below', the figure on the right 'from above'.

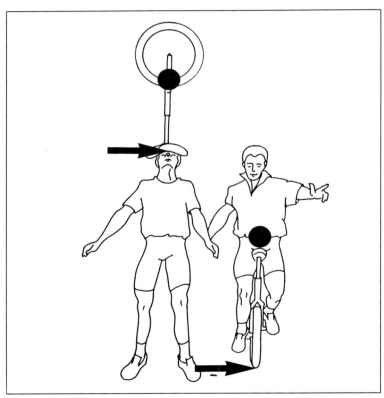

The overall centre of gravity of someone on a unicycle should lie somewhere around the hips. The whole force of gravity seems to act at this central point. To maintain balance on the unicycle, this central point must be kept over the very small point of support, i.e. the point of contact between the tyre and the ground, usually only a few square centimetres. The size of this point of contact is important. A particularly well-inflated tyre reduces the size of the contact point and makes it more difficult to keep your balance. So that balance can be maintained for longer periods on the unicycle, small correction movements must constantly be made to maintain the state of equilibrium. Since, however, the unicycle immediately wants to assume a stable balanced state again after each correction movement (ie to fall over and lie down), the next correction movement must begin immediately too.

This continual 'wobbling' to maintain balance on the unicycle causes the overall centre of gravity to sink a little. The rider-unicycle unit loses potential energy, gains kinetic energy and begins, if only a fraction, to tip over. To avoid falling, (muscle) work must be carried out and the lost potential energy (usually only minimal) is restored again through a compensatory movement. The unicyclist is therefore involved in a constant struggle to maintain balance.

Balancing objects of differing length

It is well-known that a long object is easier to balance than a short one: A broom can therefore be balanced more easily on the hand than a pencil. In terms of physics a falling pole performs a circular movement with constant angular acceleration. The longer the pole the more time is required to describe a particular angle. A long pole therefore takes longer to fall than a short one. Because of the longer 'falling time' you have more time to make corrective movements.

Since unicycling is a balancing act, it is easier in terms of physics to keep your balance on a Giraffe; here you have more time to react to the movement of the Giraffe with compensatory movements and corrections.

Falling motion of different sized unicycles. A taller unicycle takes longer to fall, you therefore have more time to make corrective movements.

Side to side rolling motion

Unicycling on railway tracks is a pointless exercise and inevitably results in a fall because to do it without even the tiniest side-to-side rolling movement is impossible. Why is this?

As you ride along, different forces act on the unicycle. Some of these are described as torque, since they cause or tend to cause rotation. Powering the unicycle, by pedalling, produces torque around the spindle at right angles to the direction of travel, contributing to the rotation of the wheel and therefore the locomotion. However, pedalling also produces torque around the axis pointing in the direction of travel. This force leads to a sideways tilting of the wheel with every downward push on the pedal. When the right pedal is pushed downwards, the whole unicycle leans a little to the right through the influence of this force. When the left pedal is pushed downwards, the unicycle leans to the left. Each time the unicycle tips in this way the tyre is at a slight angle to the ground and, because of this, is forced to make very slight curves to the left and right alternately. It is these curves strung together which cause the noticeable side to side rolling motion as you unicycle.

Since this rolling movement is the result of the inherent laws of physics you will never manage to eliminate it completely, so consequently you will not succeed in riding on railway tracks. However, it is possible to suppress the movement considerably. To do this you have to actively counter-steer with compensatory movements of your body. It is a sign of an advanced technique if you can ride the unicycle so directly forwards that you manage to keep these ever-present deviations from the straight line as small as possible, so that they are barely visible to the observer. Rolling movements occur with all wheel sizes, though with smaller wheels it is more sharply pronounced. Larger wheels behave more sluggishly and are therefore more stable against external influences.

Frictional forces

Static and rolling friction are of great significance to unicyclists. Static friction is the obstructive force encountered when two surfaces move against one another, rolling friction is the obstructive force encountered when a wheel rolls along the ground.

Static frictional forces are increased with a rough floor covering, a rough, poorly inflated tyre and a heavy rider. The result is that the unicycle is more difficult to manoeuvre. Changes of direction on the spot become particularly difficult. Conversely, the frictional forces are reduced by a smooth and well-inflated tyre and a lighter rider. The unicycle runs better and more easily due to the low rolling friction and can also be controlled more easily. However, due to the reduction in static friction, the danger of the wheel slipping from under you increases.

Rotation around the long axis

According to the laws of physics which govern action and reaction, the force applied to a body causes an effective force of the same size in the opposite direction. For example, if you sit still on a swivel chair and it is not possible to push off from something with your arms or legs, you cannot initiate a turn by yourself. Even if you twist your arms and upper body vigorously in one direction (action), the lower body turns in the opposite direction (reaction). Action and reaction cancel each other out as forces of equal size and in this way the swivel chair cannot be put in motion.

The same effect also happens with turns on a unicycle, providing the force employed is strong enough to overcome the friction between the tyre and the floor. This is usually the case if you make strong and rapid arm and upper body movements. If, for example, you move your upper body vigorously and quickly to the left, your lower body moves with the unicycle to the right. As on the swivel chair, the turn you initiate is curbed by an opposing force.

Nevertheless, it is possible to turn the unicycle on the spot from a relatively idle position without pedalling, and do a half- pirouette or even more. If you turn your upper body slowly to one side you produce only a slight force, and consequently only a small counter-force which is not sufficient to overcome the rolling friction of the tyre on the floor. In this case, the unicycle does not turn in the opposite direction. After you have turned your upper body slowly to one side, your hips and shoulders are at an angle of about 90 degrees to each other.

**The principle of action and reaction on a unicycle.
Quick and vigorous upper body movement in one direction leads
to the turning of the lower body and the unicycle
in the other direction.**

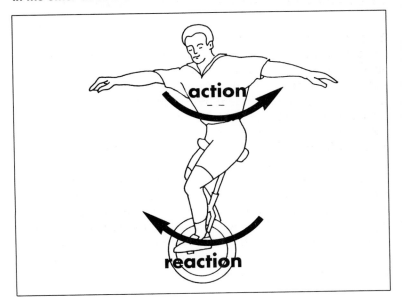

If from this position, you twist your upper body quickly in the desired direction of movement, the angular momentum generated can be transferred to both the lower body and the unicycle, enabling you to make a half-turn or more. This technique does not produce continuous rotation because the frictional forces, which make the pirouette possible only in this way, ensure that the turning movement is quickly curbed. Therefore repeated body turns are only possible if you constantly repeat the process described above, i.e. slow turn, quick twist, slow turn, quick twist etc. However, rotation is constantly broken up by the turning and twisting movement. This technique is therefore not so difficult, because the vertical axis and the axis of rotation coincide from the beginning.

Uninterrupted rotation of over 180 degrees around the vertical axis can only rarely be generated without external angular momentum. For this you can either push off from a wall or be set in motion by other people (see p.129). However, you also gain momentum for several turns by firstly riding in big circles, then ever smaller ones until you finally rotate on the spot without pedalling. When you ride in small circles the vertical axis is inclined a little to the centre of the circle. This means that in the transition to rotating on the spot the unicycle must be brought exactly upright, since the vertical axis coincides with the turning axis. This transition is one of the biggest problems when you try to initiate a pirouette. As with figure skaters, who skate in ever-decreasing circles to execute a pirouette, your arms should be kept tight to your body. Due to the fact that the mass of body and unicycle together is directed nearer to the centre of turn, inertia is reduced and the turning movement is made easier.

The History of Unicycling

The origins of unicycling have everything to do with one of the most important inventions in the history of humanity; the wheel. The invention of the wheel is traced back to around 4000 BC and often attributed to the Sumerians. It is more likely, however, that the wheel and the carriage were developed at the same time in differing parts of the old world. One of the oldest surviving portrayals of the wheel (about 3000 BC) originates from the Sumerian town of Ur, which shows it as a complete disc.

Spoked carriage wheels were a further important step in the development of the bicycle. The oldest surviving evidence of such wheels, which were attached to war-chariots, originated from the Egyptians in the 16th Century BC.

The depiction of what was probably the first two-wheeled machine also originates from Egypt (13th Century BC). A person is sitting on a kind of supporting beam which is connected by two wheels running behind one another. The diagram is located on the now heavily weather-beaten obelisk in the Place de la Concorde in Paris (Lemke/Gronen, p.9).

In the field of (uni-) cycling there was little development for centuries until in 1817 Karl Freiherr of Drais managed to build a steerable walking machine.

However, it was only through an invention by Frenchman Ernest Micheaux in 1861 that a further and extremely important breakthrough was achieved. Micheaux attached cranks to the front wheel.

It is due to him that "the feet were lifted from the ground when travelling along and the walking motion of the Drais machine was replaced by a pedalling motion" (Franke 1987, p.114). With the construction of the Micheaux-cycle the development to penny-farthing and unicycle was now clearly mapped out. Micheaux's bicycle achieved quick success and became a market leader. However, to cover long distances on this machine it was essential to pedal quickly and constantly to make any progress. Only through a large drive wheel, i.e. a large front wheel, was the rider freed from hectic pedalling when travelling fast because there was no gearing system. Enlarging the front wheel of the Micheaux-cycle and reducing the size of the rear one resulted in the penny-farthing. With this development the rear wheel became more and more a supporting wheel which some riders could and indeed wanted to forgo. The dispensing of the rear wheel on the penny-farthing probably marked the birth of the first unicycle.

With regard to the unicycle, there was still a further line of development for those designers who from the outset dreamt of being able to ride on one wheel. Most of these ingenious eccentrics did not foresee that later generations would judge their projects as follows: "If the magnitude of an invention lies in its simplicity then the unicycle must be nothing short of brilliant" (Rauck etc 1979, p.54). If the idea was brilliant, actually riding a unicycle was the problem on which the widespread success of such an invention floundered. The first machine resembling a unicycle was the 'Pédocaètre' by Frenchman M.Davis in 1853, a hand-driven vehicle for two people. In 1870 the Englishman J. Hobby built a huge unicycle, and in 1880 an Italian gym instructor built a unicycle on which he is supposed to have travelled from Milan to Turin (approx. 200km).

At this time (somewhere between 1880 and 1890) riding a penny-farthing, and particularly a unicycle, was nevertheless a pleasure enjoyed by only a few people.

Mastering a penny-farthing constituted a considerable sporting achievement. The rider's seating position was almost directly over the front axle, placing demands similar to riding a unicycle on the skill of the rider.

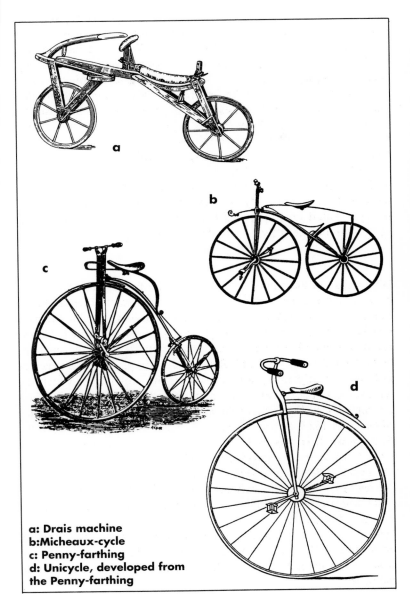

a: Drais machine
b:Micheaux-cycle
c: Penny-farthing
d: Unicycle, developed from
the Penny-farthing

a: Pédocaètre,
b: J.Hobby's unicycle
c: Scuris cycle, the independent development into the unicycle

"Consequently the penny-farthing remained the domain of young, athletic men. At 20 to 25 km/hr it was twice as fast as the pioneering velocipedes or cranked cycles which preceded it" (Franke 1987, p.14). To ride a penny-farthing you needed something extra special which distinguished you from the masses: "There is no doubt that the increased risk which the ambitious penny-farthing riders ran also contributed to their pride and self-esteem. For them the penny-farthing was to low machines what the bicycle is to a bone-shaker. Consequently riding a penny-farthing was artistry... If one follows this artistic line, the unicycle is actually the most logical outcome; it is the most unstable machine and requires nothing other than the art of maintaining balance. On a bicycle this is no problem for most people; ...however, the unicycle demands acrobats. Psychologically, it is quite understandable that large groups of potential cyclists have not participated in this step upward" (Krausse 1987, p.45).

Therefore, it becomes clear that firstly the development from penny-farthing to unicycle, and secondly the independent development of the unicycle, have played only a minor role in the history of the bicycle. The main development of the bicycle was the transfer of the chain drive to the back wheel, thus resulting in the development of the 'standard' two-wheeler. The great success of the two-wheeler condemned the penny-farthing and the unicycle to the status of dangerous and unappealing relics.

In the last decade of the previous century the penny-farthing and the tall unicycle (Giraffe) enjoyed a brief heyday and the ability of trick cyclists like Nick Kaufmann (USA), Auguste Gouget (France) and Gustav Marschner (Germany) was legendary at the time. At various competitions the one-wheel performers competed against each other (see illustrations, p.168/169). Some tricks clearly suggest that quite a few unicycle techniques developed from riding a penny-farthing.

Were Kaufmann to have moved on the wheel in his second demonstration (see drawing p.169, centre top) and not just stood on top of it (as he appears to be doing), this could well have been one of the first illustrations of wheel-walking. Kaufmann's third trick shows that riding on one wheel was also possible without modifications to the penny-farthing.

**Competitive trick-cycling in the Albert Hall of the Crystal Palace at
Leipzig on March 6th 1892 during the Sports Festival of the
Saxony Cycling Association (Illustrirte Zeitung, March 19th 1892)**

Contest for the Trick-cycling Championship of Europe in 1894 in Leipzig (Illustrirte Zeitung, March 10th 1894). Illustrations 1-6, demonstrations by Kaufmann; Illustrations 7-10, by Gouget.

Even a century ago unicyclists were not only measuring their trick-cycling skills; races were also organised exclusively for unicycles, as here in Greiz (Eastern Germany), 1886.

Racing, however, was not supposed to have been very comfortable. At that time unicycles were still equipped with solid rubber tyres - air-filled rubber tyres from Dunlop and Michelin only became widespread in the 1890's.

The end of the 19th Century also saw the end of the 'wild time' of cycle development, a time of experimentation, of trials and tests, of racing and competitions without hard and fast rules, a time which also produced many other creative and curious inventions in unicycle development. Certainly the 'tinkerers', the DIY constructors and the ingenious and eccentric engineers never shied away from the risk of testing out their own designs.

By the end of the 19th Century, the two-wheeled cycle had proved to

Wheel-removal. Most of the early unicycles could not deny their origin from the penny-farthing. Firstly the supporting wheel and the saddle were removed (left, unicyclist Felix Brunner, Munich), then later the frame with handlebars as well, leaving just the wheel with cranks and pedals (above, Arthur Streubel, Leipzig).

be far superior. In 1903, the first Tour de France was a huge success. There was hardly any demand for penny-farthings or unicycles, and in the following decades the skill of riding one or the other gradually faded into oblivion. The new machine even caught on with trick cyclists, and today competitions are still held exclusively for bicycles. Nevertheless, the art of riding on one wheel is still kept up by trick cyclists, though usually performed on bicycles.

In the following years the art of unicycling was mostly limited to a few colourful individuals who developed it into a circus skill. The triumphal march of the bicycle also considerably affected the construction of unicycles - the wheels were built with smaller, more standard dimensions and soon resembled those on unicycles as they are built today.

Adolf Günter poses after his record of 200 kilometres on a unicycle around the Bodensee (Germany). Apart from the handlebars, this unicycle from 1910 already resembles those of the modern day.

Appendix

Bibliography

Altig, Rudi / Link, Karl: Optimale Radsporttechnik 1: Grundlagen. Oberhaching 1985.

August, Helga: Kleines Lexikon der Superlative. München 1989.

Böhm, Ludwig / Born, Hans: Das Kunstradfahren. Tenningen 1976.

Franke, Jutta: Illustrierte Fahrrad-Geschichte, Materialien. Museum für Verkehr und Technik. Berlin 1987.

Freiwald, Jürgen: Aufwärmen im Sport. Reinbek bei Hamburg 1991.

Grosser, M. / Neumaier, A.: Techniktraining. München, Wien, Zurich 1982.

Hotz, A. / Weineck, J.: Optimales Bewegungslernen. Erlangen 1988.

Huisman, Bennie und Gerard: Akrobatik. Vom Anfänger zum Könner. Reinbek bei Hamburg 1988.

Knebel, Karl-Peter: Funktionsgymnastik. Reinbek 1985/1991.

Krausse, Joachim: Velo-Evolution, in: Wietzer, Rolf / Schmidt, Maruta (Red.): FahrradLiebe. Berlin 1987.

Kukla, D. : Radsport, in: Pförringer, W. / Rosemeyer, B / Bär, H.-W. (Hg.): Sporttraumatologie. Erlangen 1981.

Kümmel, H.-H.: Das neue Guinness Buch der Rekorde. Frankfurt a.M./ Berlin 1990.

Lemke, W. / Gronen, W.: Geschichte des Radsports und des Fahrrads von den Anfängen bis 1939. Eupen 1978.

de Marées, H. / Mester, J.: Sportphysiologie I. Frankfurt a.M. 1981.

Rauck, M. / Volke, G. / Paturi, F.: Mit dem Rad durch zwei Jahrhunderte. Aarau / Stuttgart 1979.

Syer, John / Connolly, Christopher: Psychotraining für Sportler. Reinbek bei Hamburg 1988.

Wiley, Jack: The Complete Book of Unicycling. Lodi, California 1984.

Zorn, Henk: Radsport. Reinbek bei Hamburg 1991.

Unicycle Manufacturers

DM Engineering,
59 Fairmile Road,
Christchurch,
Dorset, BH23 2LA,
England

Sem Abrahams Engineering,
P.O. Box 1675,
3600 BR Maarssen,
Holland

D. & G. Siegmon,
Rodenbeker Weg 3,
2300 Kiel,
Germany

Pichler Radtechnik,
Steinstr. 23, Gewerbehof
7500 Karlsruhe,
Germany

Photo Sources

Bildarchiv Preußischer Kulturbesitz: Pages 168, 169
Armin Bittner: Page 11
German Museum, Munich: Pages 166 (b) and (c)
DM Engineering/ DM Ringmaster Unicycles: Pages 14, 16
International Juggling Archive, Karl-Heinz Ziethen: Pages 152, 153
Joachim Krausse: Page 165
Pichler Radtechnik: Pages 133, 135
Radsport-Archiv, Wolfgang Gronen: Pages 23, 166 (a), 170, 171 (2), 172
Dagmar Siegmon (Siegmono Cycle): Page 20
The Walt Disney Company Ltd: Pages 13, 21
Gerd Waree: Page 111

The Author

Sebastian Höher (born 1953) studied Sport at the Free University in Berlin and teaches Sport at a Berlin grammar school. After a period pursuing achievement-orientated sports (he was German Karate Champion and a member of the national team, among other things), he sought a new sporting challenge and found this firstly in juggling, then later in unicycling. Initially, he taught himself to unicycle, noting down his practice exercises at each stage of the learning process. Through his acquaintance with Eckhard Euen, an outstanding unicyclist, he learnt many of the finer points of unicycling. In addition to learning and practising himself, Sebastian Höher has taught many other people to unicycle. In this way he has constantly been able to develop and refine his methods, the nucleus of which are his numerous and diverse practice exercises.

For up to date information on where to buy unicycles and how to contact other unicyclists, see the following magazines:

Britain & Europe

The Catch
Subscriptions: Moorlegde Farm Cottage, Knowle Hill,
Chew Magna, Bristol, BS18 8TL.

Germany & Europe

Kaskade
Subscriptions: Annastrasse 7, D65197
Wiesbaden, Germany.

U.S.A.

Jugglers' World
Subscriptions: I.J.A. Box 218, Montague
WA01351 U.S.A.